DECADENCE
and
GREEK

By the same author

PLAYS

SHORT STORIES

PLAYSCRIPT 103

DECADENCE
and
Greek

Steven Berkoff

JOHN CALDER · LONDON
RIVERRUN PRESS · NEW YORK

This volume first published in Great Britain 1982 by
John Calder (Publishers) Ltd
18 Brewer Street, London W1R 4AS

and first published in the USA 1983 by
Riverrun Press Inc.
1170 Broadway, New York, NY 10001

Second Impression 1986

Decadence was first published privately by the author in 1981
and *Greek* was also published by the author in 1980
© Steven Berkoff 1980, 1982, 1983, 1986

British Library Cataloguing in Publication Data
Berkoff, Steven
  Decadence; and Greek. — (Playscripts; 103)
  I. Title
  822'.914   PR6052.E588

ISBN 0 7145 3954 6 paperbound

Typeset in 9/10 pt Times
Printed in Great Britain by Hillman Printers (Frome) Ltd.

CONTENTS

Decadence

For Helen

Decadence was first performed at the New End Theatre, Hampstead, London, on 14 July, 1981.

The cast was as follows:

HELEN	Linda Marlowe
STEVE	Steven Berkoff
SYBIL	Linda Marlowe
LES	Steven Berkoff
Director	Steven Berkoff
Designer	Mani Fagenblum
Lighting	Howard Harrison
Stage Manager	Dani Lukic

ACT ONE

Scene One

Black floor. A white set. Woman in black. Man in black and white. A woman sits on a white leather sofa. Music plays, a forties' Ambrose record. A man in tails and wing collar stands near her in a pose of frozen upper class glee. He remains frozen until he speaks apart from lighting her cigarette. All cigarettes and drinks are mimed with great emphasis to extract the greatest amount of absurdity from the physical response. Acting should be sensual, erotic, flamboyant.

HELEN.   How sweet of you to come on time / bastard! sweet darling! my you do look so divine. I've been so bored / have a drink / what . . . ? / Of course! a drambui with soda and a splash of cinzano . . . with masses of ice / I've been so bored tearing round to find just what would enchant you to eat me for breakfast *(raising skirt)* charmant n'est-ce pas / does it make you go all gooey / does it send spasms up and down your spine / enough ice! sweety you do look nice. Do you like my legs? / aren't my frillies sweet / does it make you get just a little on heat / kiss me / gently / don't smudge now / just a touch / a graze won't be a trice / I'll get ready / so late I couldn't find a fucking taxi / oh I hate to miss the first scene the first embrace / what's that we're seeing / the name of the play! / taxis were thin on the ground / outside Harrods there were none around / I stretched out an arm / I felt like Moses / what did he do / raise his arms to heaven for the Hebrews / the longer he kept his arm in the air the better would his armies fare, but when it fell wearily down / bloody nosed moishers and crunch smash and pound / you've not said a word / but you do look dishy / a bird in the ice floes / or chilled meringue frappe / you look simply gay / got a fag . . . hmm! Smoke gets in your eyes! Shit! Oh sorry / tit! Ready heart? Where for dinner after / surprise me then, give me a thrill / so long as I gorge on some juicy meat / I'm as hungry as a vampire / if I don't eat soon I'll simply expire / did you have a nice day / little wife all safe and tucked away / come open your mouth and dazzle my ears / come love . . . / you look troubled / close to tears / what have I done . . . shit . . . you look bad / what's the matter hone(y)?

STEVE.   So bleeding dexterous / wouldn't you know / too much bloody ice love / tastes like a crow / you ask me the cause for my down face / wait till you hear what I have to say / unzip your ears and let me flood them with verbs and make your mind a jangle of nerves / the bloody slut got cute / decided for a hunch to hire a dick with a nose like a jew / a private detective in case you're not yet clued / to follow me here / and now I fear the game's up my dear / the bloody bitch got wise when too many spunkless nights rolled by / it made her think that I was not emptying my tea pot in her old kitchen sink /

HELEN.   Oh fuck darling

STEVE.   You've said a mouthful there

HELEN. Don't worry darling / you've nothing to fear / say your hard on's taking a small holiday this year / the work and strain of conning your way in this world sends the cock to the brain / her jealousies are painted shadows / relieve her pain / and drop a morsel or two in your old dame / but a private dick / that's a hell of a game!

STEVE.   Too bloody true Helen / my god you're a beaut / a fabulous sight / I could feast my eyes on you day and night / let's go out on the town / fuck this dick / let's go and get tight / but damn this greasy bleeder if he's outside he'll follow us / there's nowhere to hide / then it's all out / the evidence clear / he'll tell her all there is needed to hear.

HELEN.   Is chartreuse with pink just too too much / my head is spining darling / what did you say / are you sure you're not fantasising / did you have a bad day / I don't know what to wear / help me darling don't just stand there.

STEVE.   Let me make it clear / let me shake up the slop that tries to pretend it's a brain not a mop / my dearest wife Sybil, this morning she said / if I don't stop whoring I'm just as well dead / now try and get that in your fucking head! A divorce and it's ample she has all the clues / photos no doubt / it will make all the news / cut off / not a penny / as broke as a mouse / no fortune no wages / and she keeps the house / got a light?

HELEN.   So what shall we do? / Oh Stevie / it's beastly what she does to you / is my seam straight / oh come on darling we mustn't be late /

STEVE.   You don't seem to realise this beast is trailing my scent / I can't think / my hard on's getting quite bent / to feel this creature so close on my back / spying, reporting my every track / I can just see him now / can't you / putting two and two together to the bloody cow /

Scene Two

LES *and* SYBIL *(same actors change attitude and positions)*

LES.   So, I followed him to this sumptuous flat / a conspiracy is what I make of that /

SYBIL.   Wadya mean a conspiracy? / To fucking wot? /

LES.   Wak your treasure! Your old man's sticking his nasty in some horrible / birds of a fucking feather ducky stick to fucking gether / these ex public schools well grounded in making fools of us / the country's pus that welts up from the blood and guts of me and you / you married the cunt / when your old dad said at the time / he's just a runt / just after your considerable dough / which dad's sweated his balls off for and now you bunged it to some male whore / set up no doubt in pad / contributed by your not inconsiderable swag / it makes you double choke / this ponce swishes you off your plates of meat / down Blakes or Tramps or other swishy hole / where half assed bastards and criminals go / the foul / ignoble mob / odd judge MP and law sniff round the seamy door / liking what's on the other side of the swamp / have a romp / Incognito and hope that what's for dough will taste better than old Flo in curlers / rancid in East Cheam / and when they've had their bit of fun / head home again all nice for Flo / who's lying in a heap of cream and wax / clutching Cosmopolitan or other crap / with overfed pussy on her lap.

SYBIL.   And I don't want to get like that / thanks love / I feel a little better now / when I found out / I'll kill the fucking cow I thought / at first / you know how you do / I cried for days / right broke up / never dreamed that my dear Steve would do that to me / the big question is why / ours is not to reason but to die / that's how I felt / but now I'm calmed and like the sea all tempest tossed / you're thrown this way and that / like being screwed if you like by some big black cat / you can't think for the storm shoved up / but after in the trough of calm / thoughts that seem wise gather round / counsel me to nothing rash / be clever Sybil / don't go mad / the taste is sweet when you're stabbing guts in heat / but later in cold cell / there's too much time to dwell / but do it neat / cut off his money and you may as well cut off his feet / he won't move / he can't / he's helpless like his kind / no drive within / no chin to take the blows that come at him /

LES.   Ata girl / that's how I like to see you chat / like some fucking great jungle cat / claws withdrawn ready to pounce and rip apart this paltry mouse / quiet as death still as a stone / then pow! Tear his flesh off his bones / that's what we do / take our time / don't frite the bastard he'll shit his pipe / let him be forgiven / don't do it again darling / slip powdered glass in his gin / I seen a guy who swallowed glass / I seen the blood pour out of his ass and out of his ears / vomit it up in cups of mashy red / the simple conclusion / he's better off dead!

SYBIL.   You're crazy Les I swear / don't do nothing daft / he knows about you dear /

LES.   What! You've told him about me / shit! Now you've blown my little fantasy!

SYBIL.   He only thinks I hired a private dick / but one familiar for whom I lick his prick / but I disturbed one day by ill concealed traces of some sexual play / some love tattoos left in his flies / he thinks I hired a pair of eyes / not realising that I was on to anything more strong than a vibrator when he's on his trips so long / and now I know that those business trips were dirty business to see his trick / greasy joints and my dough to help cream the way / they say money's the best lubricator / no need for K.Y.

LES.   You sound just great / I could eat you up / you look like a lioness / I feel like your cub / take your knickers off I wanna fuck /

SYBIL.   Tell you the truth / I'd rather have a suck!

Scene Three

STEVE *and* HELEN *(they melt into the characters as before)*

STEVE *(smoking).*   Do you know I never saw my old dad / maybe on weekends sometime / or end of term / he'd come over with mum in a toni perm / prize giving / that was it / I never got nothing / a prize nitwit / then we'd go to lunch / sit in a bloody restaurant / a tight horrid bunch of us / all quite like a church and all the other kids with dads and mums pretending it was such fun to see your mum once in three months / a fiver in your pocket and chin up Steve / write to us Colin / work hard Pete / give us a call when you feel the need / cheers love / the Jaguar bites the gravel and tears away in the dust / hands wave from the back / you bite and gulp / feel tears about to start / they're off to somewhere hot / to Monte Carlo for the season / dad's a whizz at bridge and both of them like to dance but never taught me a game of cards that I might join them in their nights of laughs / that I heard from other rooms / when I in bed all alone would moan / these were the days before public school darling or poofs palace for the sons of fools / when I was still a thing to be shunted around / don't make a sound / don't spoil their play / just laughter from other rooms and wet long days / and then the drive to bloody P. school and farewell home forever really / you'll love it here he said / rugger, cross country runs / will make the man of me / he wants so much to be / see you / spring summer autumn winter / and each time the absence makes the heart grow colder / more restrained and still the bloody mid term restaurants / you are looking older Steve / and how's the game / you still wing three quarters? / Here's a fiver / shove it in your pocket / so when the P.T. master showed a friendly eye I warmed to him / and when he put his hand on my thigh / it didn't feel so bad 'cause I missed dad / or man / or somehow had / to unite with someone not to feel sad / so at first it's just a little wank / all friendly / just a dirty prank / start looking forward to it now and getting good at it myself / and then one day he asked me to stick it in / right up his ass / I felt a little queer I must confess but after it felt fine / just like a cunt / funny that / could be a juicy tart / if you shut your eyes and put your mind on snatch well after I opened flies like sardine cans / and public school / it taught me this / that buggery can be total bliss / some poor small frightened fag / protect him and you've got his bum for life / well, so one day headmaster strolls in when I'm giving head / and says Forsyth / you're dead / get out this school you filthy scum / I won't have these things going on / just pack your bags / this is not a school for fags / he wrote to dad / to say your son likes nothing better than a school boy's bum and would he come up and collect the scum / you see the school was rife / so thick in queers you could have cut it with a knife / but dad was too ashamed to think he sired a bloody poof / and sent

instead the chauffeur down to pick me up / who must have got wind somehow of my deed / since after driving for some time / he stopped along a country lane / and said / you're not to blame / these schools are cesspits of male
vice / but I suppose it is sometimes rather nice / it doesn't make you bent as a
hairpin / to indulge sometimes in a little sin / I've got two kids your age
myself he said / and put his hand right on my prick / and when it got as hard
as rock / he winked and gave it a bit of a lick / bloody hell he turned me round
and shoved it right up my kyber pass / fuck you I thought / I've had enough /
so dad said when at home / you disgust me / you perve / dirty little homo /
reptile and foul bandit for turds / take that / and with his fist delivered a
mighty whack / which missed / since I boxed somewhat at school and knew a
thing or two about Queensbury rules / I didn't just hold prefects' tools / I had
enough somehow from men / and all my hate welled up for him / don't do it
dad I said / and smashed a right hand on his nose / which forth with began to
sprout a rose / I then curled hard my other fist and put it on his jaw / mother
screamed and dad looked very ill / but do you know / it gave me quite a thrill
to beat my dad up / suddenly my pain just went away / and that was the last
time I was gay / I don't regret it though I'm glad to say / I think the dads of this
world carry a lot of blame . . . .

HELEN. So darling / what's new? / You lay back like a cow / all fat and
cuddy and relate the news of your distant past / of your distress at home with
nasty old pa / the tape unwinds / the story starts afresh / and as you speak
you seem to lay back in a bath / you wallow in a trough of all your suffering
and woe / prattle on / take out a cigarrette and . . . go! / And dad did this to
me and that / and he said this to me and that / and he **never** gave me this or
that / when I was young and needy / little wretch more like and greedy / with
an ego like a hole that never can be filled / until it sucked the very air from out
their mouths / and on and on the never ending tape of dad and mum / and
why you're like you are / the scars from wounds that open fresh showing their
tincts of blood / whenever I or other by mishap should graze that precious
weal / that you are not too keen to heal / that you so covetously keep so you
can whine afresh and weep my dad did this to me / he never took me to the
football match / deprived you pet and mum gave you a hiding / so you kept
your little treasure chest of grief / that you would open when you want to
peek at your old little pains / and multiply a little grief that lasted seconds into
a bible of woe is me / makes us all read the boring text and thus excuse yourself of all your crimes / just because life's been so unkind / when you can't
think, or grow a little bored with how or what to do / the unused precious
energy now feeds on you / frustrated in other words / starts fishing out dead
herrings of past hurts / and waves them hot and smelly from their long
sojourn. / Throw out these stinking fish / don't use another soul to listen to
your ancient threadbare woes / you crave for new fresh birds that can fill
chock full / unroll again your scroll of agony for them / and then you want
new talents / new assaults to taste because you've nothing more to say / how
many ways of cooking that old stew / get on your stomach darling *(she starts
massaging his back)* but live now in the present / perceive what's outside you
bring home your tales of raw today / and what I'm feeling now / all the hurts
accept / nay welcome since they are fresh fish from the ocean / cut off the

past that you drag by a rope like some old ship carrying cargoes of junk and waste then you'll be light, weightless and fast not tied like Ulysses to a mast / afraid to hear unchained the Sirens blast / afraid of the unknown / kill off the kid and be full grown / with me your sack is empty / so feverishly you scratch at some other unsuspecting pair of ears / till they say ow! Enough! I can't take any more / then on you go / the ancient mariner or wandering Jew who must unload his slops and spew / live in the now / and pain and past will crumble fast in sweet fresh air / like ancient mummies dead for years in darkened vaults just fall apart when light and air expose their fetid lair / don't drag your ma and pa from out their graves to bail you out for all the shit / it's you now boy / if the shoe fits . . .

STEVE.   Wear it / it's so true *(he starts to grope her)*

HELEN.   Stop it!

STEVE.   Darling . . .

HELEN.   Stop it!

STEVE.   Darling . . .

HELEN.   Stop i i i it!!

STEVE.   O.K. darling

They both sit on couch — he looks suitably abashed.

STEVE.   Truce?

HELEN *(silence).*

STEVE.   Love you!

HELEN *(silence).*

STEVE. Lurve you!

HELEN *(silence).*

STEVE. Luurrve yoouu!

HELEN.   O.K. Love you

This continues for a moment more — STEVE *sits back happy and contented.*

STEVE.   Mustn't feel sorry for myself / but I do get bored darling waiting for you / to come home and cheer me up / give me a laugh / you're super jolly good at that / not bloody half / a sense of humour / that's a treat / that's what is vital to our love / I think / can't bear humourless people / the ones who think, the ones who think their shit don't stink / still you're right about me love / you've hit it on the nail I do repeat the same old tale / I think I told that story every time / to every different woman of mine / and like a player on the stage / repeating the same life every day / repetition wears the brain away / what's my stars say? Any fortune or some fame along the way / some foreign travel . . . what! My love life is so perfect so there's nothing there / couldn't be better poppet / love you darling / my super wondrous piece of dolly arse /

my dishy lovely slice of peach melba / pour me a gin and it / no make it a scotch and dry / I fancy that / and then / no parties anywhere tonight / ring Alex would you or old Keith / he'll have a rubber or gin rummy going / bless him, he's a card / raced his Ferrari last week 'gainst Claude's Lamborghini and both bloody collided / pissed myself laughing / you think Keith gave a fart / no fear / that's fucking fixed that one / let's go and get another / and damn me if the blighter didn't just go and buy a bloody new one / what a card / there's too much bloody ice in here you wicked nymph / it takes so long to train them nowadays / what's for dinner darling / something new / surprise me / I'm so bloody bored with filet / tastes like rubber nowadays / what's in the bloody feed I wonder, plastic chippings I've no doubt / oh let's book up at Fred's / that's very you / a sole bonne femme or strogonoff or even a fondue / another drink my sweet / love you darling / you o.k.? / You seem a little pinched / what's up my lollipop eh? / What's a-matter little lollypop / does you want papa to take your little drawers down and pin you to the sofa / oh don't look like that / like I'm something just brought in by the cat / o.k. I'm off the beam tonight but feel a little twitchy down there / thought to pass the time . . . n'est-ce pas / petit divertissement / no? / That's just fine with me / lovely legs you've got / they go right up and up and get lost up your bum / ooops mustn't get a hard on / just when we are going out / eh love / fancy a tickle with the old giggle stick / no, o.k. / you used to get weak at the knees just at the suggestion / cream your jeans / you used to say / I suppose you take me now for granted, eh! / But I'm so bloody bored tonight / don't know the cause / maybe I'm reaching male menopause / what do you think ? I'm only joking dear / don't look like you smell some awful stink.

Scene Four

Lights fade. Come up on SYBIL *and* LES.

SYBIL.   So how's the plot / what's happening / what's the plan / are you still with me my desperate Dan / powdered glass or poison in his drink / what's better / what do you think? /

LES.   It's hard to tell / fuck only knows / poison leaves traces in his gut / and clues that may point back to you my pet / don't make things worse by sewing seeds that may sprout later as evil deeds that tend to boomerang and whack you down / kick out the bastard / get rid of the clown / that's my advice / get your mouth round that.

Scene Five

Mood is from prior scene. Lights fade— come up on HELEN *and* STEVE.

STEVE.   I don't know why I'm so bored /

HELEN.   Oh let me cheer you up.

STEVE.   Would you?

HELEN.   It's very simple — you're a pup who needs a game to keep his spirits
all /

STEVE.   Yeees!

HELEN.   I'll tell you a story — once upon a time / you just lie there and I'll be
Scheherazade / let me beguile your ears with tales to ravish you my dear /

STEVE.   Let's have a cigarette first

HELEN.   O.K.

They light cigarettes and they both have hysterical fun blowing smoke rings.

HELEN.   The morning's sun was high up in the sky / a great big orange in a sea
of blue / and caw caws from the fluffy floating gulls, and yachts were thick as
icing in the breathless still and crispy morning / the wind as soft as shantung
whispers / the windows from my hotel room lay open and the curtains softly
waved from time to time / the bed as white as arctic snows and little bells
would tinkle from the yachts to tickle in your ears and wake you up / the
servants softly tread down corridors thick pile with chink of coffee cups and
clutching morning papers thickly folded / little gentle taps on doors / the
knuckle's light morse code to wake the wealthy from their night long doze,
while swallowed in silk sheets and thick duvets in darkened curtained rooms
they lay / fat and white giant slugs, stirring with parched and furry mouth
anxious for their morning cups / the room still drenched in stale cigar smoke
while their stomach's lining burns in torment still from last night's bloated fill
/ mignon stuffed with oysters / caviar and crêpe suzette, lobster thermidor
and poisoned liver of wild ducks / the brains of pigs in aspic laced with the
tongue of sheep in the blood of nightingales / garlic crushed in veal whose
occupants were shut in boxes from their birth and fed with milk to be more
tender / their flesh so soft it hurts / so in their fat cocoons they lay in half som-
nolent daze / the bathroom scattered like jewels with multitudes of coloured
pills / the clothes lay in a heap, my watch from Cartier. Good time it keeps /
lay on the side / with a glass of champagne, half drunk, warm and tacky now /
all that had been so sweet the night before / looked in the morning like death
and gore / the plates not gathered by room service looked a foul and fetid
mess / and then the servant bless him all crisp and white came like an angel / a
blessed sight / a soft tap on the door / like a whisper / like a plea / to be
allowed to serve the tea / and not disturb / come in I said and lay your
treasures by my bed / your silver tray and pot all steaming hot / and crois-
sants crisp and soft and twirls of butter / coloured sugar like broken glass /
honey and the Paris Match / he gathered up the last night's dregs and cleared
the room / made it sweet and clean again / removed the clues of last night's
greed when guts were stuffed with sensual things / and then I breathed / to
pay him for his chore / to give a tip I turned around to wake the bore / the
beast I came with / but he was dead asleep / I could not find a franc for the
young and pretty man / so there he stood like some Apollo waiting to be dis-
missed but still stood near the bed / like he was waiting for a gentle kiss / the

tray he held so tight / his knuckles went quite white / stood in humble supplication / ready to spin on his heel and exit at my will / I raised a hand / just enough to say / don't go yet / please stay / he caught something that I had planted in my eye / an inclined arch of eyebrow gently raised suggested . . . something / something sweet / I could almost feel his body's heat. At last I fumbled in my purse and found a franc / the corpse next to me snored and turned around / the boy stood still / as stiff as rock / the thing that I had planted from my eyes to his / he now returned / it gave me a tiny shock / but not too much to stop my hand from wandering up / I placed it like a breath upon the inside of his leg / which felt like marble angels carved by Donatello / still he held the tray / and since the beast was snoring deep I opened the servant's flies and put my hand down deep inside until I found a large warm penis which couldn't hide / he withdrew a touch, not much / a trifle scared perhaps of monster waking and then scenarios of losing needed job / but then I flashed a pleading look / as if to say it's fun / the old man will not wake / he caught my look and bravely stayed / and gently began to squeeze his hips and buttocks / so when I took him in my mouth it was a gorgeous thrill to do it there with bastard still snoring in his lair / and then he thrust and squirted fine silk jets of come and nearly dropped the tray / the beast next door me waked / but slowly like a drunken pig / surfacing through mud / the boy retrieved his shrunken shark / turned on his heel / and made a quick depart / I meanwhile swallowed fast / then Harry woke / 'Good morning darling' I sweetly slurred / Did you sleep well? he said like bliss and fastened on my mouth a faggy kiss / my god I thought he tastes like hell.

STEVE.   How decadent darling / how simply fab divine and rare to gobble the waiter with your husband lying there / how splendid spiffing whizzo fab and gear / it's the most enchanting story that ever I did hear / you amaze me, stun, astound / Oh! Wait till this story goes around / what a plot, what an amazing scene / let's put it in a play / no one would believe it anyway / no you can't say those / those nasty words on stage / you'll have the Tory mothers in a spitting rage / oh shit, regardez l'heure / we simply mustn't be late / the play starts at a quarter to eight.

HELEN.   What are we seeing darling / what's my treat tonight?

STEVE.   A play about some filthy soldiers sticking their ends up some poor tyke.

HELEN.   How fabulous / how simply great / I want to see that / I just can't wait / all those dishy soldiers in the raw with cocks a-flashing everywhere / how simply shocking / how awfully bizarre / to train at RADA then at last when you're a full fledged actor / 'what speech will you do today' / you turn around and bare your arse / he'll do / a three year contract at Waterloo / I love all that / that blood and gore / to shock us pink and crave for more / do they do it for real darling / eight times a week?

STEVE.   No stupid / or their asses would be sore / they **act** the buggering / it's an Equity law /

HELEN.   Oh darling what a bloody bore / give me realism that's what I'm paying for!

He throws her on sofa and dives on top.

Light fades and they come up from clinch as SYBIL *and* LES.
As they come up from their embrace:-

Scene Six

LES.   Was that all right for you?

SYBIL.   Yeah — it was great. Was it all right for you?

LES.   Yeah — lovely . . . do you enjoy it?

SYBIL.   Yeah . . . it was . . . nice . . . did you?

LES.   Wo?

SYBIL.   Enjoy it!

LES.   Yeah — it was handsome.

SYBIL.   Les . . .

LES.   Wo?

SYBIL.   You don't love me no more.

LES.   Why say that?

SYBIL.   It's a fact.

LES.   If I cut off his head, is my love intact?

SYBIL.   It shows a willingness, it shows a fact.

LES.   A mug an all / a dozy git to put himself right in the shit / kick out the cunt / cut off his gelt / put him in limbo / set him loose in the world / stained, dishonoured / a con man known by all / not a leg to stand on / not even a ball / he won't even show his mug to mum as she sits in shame in the bingo hall.

SYBIL.   It don't satisfy me / it chokes me to here *(throat)* to think of that pig out in the strasser dear / stealing more dough / conning some sweet / sucking on her innocent white teat / till he's drained her dry the cunning thief / the bloated vampire / let's extinguish the creep /

LES.   You are a one / you are a hag / a right vicious tough old slag / but give me time and then I'll prove I'm twice the bloke you think / kiss me you luscious dolly pink and bouncy / you're a doll / you make me randy.

SYBIL.   You're getting back your desperate dan so don't be mean / you know how much I love you so / you're big and strong / ooh your arms are huge / then hold me tight and make me ooze you filthy bastard / touch me doll /

stick your hand inside me coat / feel my nipple / hard as rocks / oh sugar I'm just aching for your . . . .

LES.   Cor blimey, shush / you're putting me off / my mind's ablaze with violent acts inspired by your need for facts / I'll prove I love you / I'll make you see just how wondrous thou art to me / I'll measure my love in deeds so cute / I'll make de Sade go back to school / first of all one night / he comes home / stops the car, alights / my car's just behind and rams him down and pastes him to the side / he needs unpeeling so intense will be my hard caress / in bed one night / he's with his whore / there'll be a little tapping on the door / he, careful as a skunk thinking his trail has left no trace of stink / peeps through the spyhole / and sees me / costumed as a telegram boy / all safe he thinks and opens up / a ten inch blade dives in his gut / at his squash club / he's had his game / all sweaty in his shower / innocent and tame / in the steam no one sees a furtive me drop a tarantula in his pants / he dries off / dresses and suddenly shrieks / there's something up his kyber pass and it feels to me like broken glass / 'cause tarantula bite is a vicious sight / or a bomb under the lovers' bed / ready to go off as she or he comes / a neat device so sensitive / that extra pressure will blow them to shreds / they'll fly / that's an orgasm that will send them to paradise / gun's too messy and far too noisy / let's leave that out and choose a poison / we'll send him a Christmas cake juiced up with cyanide / lots of sherry to help disguise the bitter acrid taste that burns his guts / she'll scream in pain / they'll wait as death starts digging inside their brain / or, excuse me, what's the time? hydrochloric acid in his eyes / he screams / then in the dark / a fine needle penetrates his heart / he didn't see it / so in his dying breath he cannot identify Mr. Death / a minute atomic bomb the size of a pearl / a present in a ring from his golden girl timed to go off whenever you will / as the mood takes you ka boom ka blast ke pling! In africa from leper colony I extract from a native a deadly smear / then lace his shaver / one morning you'll hear / Oh I've scratched myself darling / smile and count down the minutes my dear / best of all I'll loose some rats whose fangs have been dipped in a deadly unction / one small bite and the cunt won't function / longer than it takes to drop down dead / it also saves disposing of the corpse since the rats will eat the lot of course / so whatyathink — you make your choice dove / it's just to show you what I feel **is love!**

SYBIL.   Ah darling now I know you care / a little attention makes a girl all yours / kiss me sweetheart

LES.   Pull off your drawers

Fade out and come up on STEVE *and* HELEN.

Scene Seven

STEVE.   What are you doing tomorrow darling?

HELEN.   Hunting.

STEVE.　How absolutely super/marvellous and fabulous — can I come!

HELEN.　Just me and the horse!

STEVE.　I bet you're a jolly good rider

HELEN.　You want to practise with me . . . be the horse? . . .

STEVE.　What! Can I?

HELEN.　Of course. You get down on the carpet . . . .

He does so and she smacks his bum a few times before she starts speech.

The Chase

HELEN.　The morning hung crisp over the village like a Chanel voile gown or a bouclé ruffle / hunting is so fucking thrilling / if you haven't done it / it's like explaining a fuck to the pope / do you know what I mean? it's the togetherness / the meeting at the morning pub / the stomp of horses and that lovely bloody smell / the preparation, pulling those fucking jodhpurs on / bloody hell they can be tight after a binge the previous night hello Claude and what ho Cecil! There's Jeremiah and Quentin / Jennifer / Vanessa darling you do look fab / that jacket fits you like a glove / the asses of the men look small and pretty bouncing on their steaming steeds / snorting from their sculptored snouts / what a sight / off we go, we shout / the leader of the hounds sounds his horn / they're straining hard 'gainst the curbing leash / a pack of hate / bursting to get free / dying to get that nasty little beast / yoiks and tally ho and onwards we shall go / the bloody fox let loose he scampers out all keenly in the bush / he has a bloody good time / a jolly taste of pure excitement / who doesn't like a smashing race? / The leader sounds the horn the scent's been picked up / dashed good form/ heels dig in ribs the horses swing to face the direction of the horn's sweet ring / on we go over hill and dale / watching for the bloody foxy fox's tail / gosh Cynthia's fallen in the muck / bloody bad luck! / over the brook / dash over the stream / my pounding steed's just one with me / it's hard / the saddle chafes / its tough / my pussy feels delightful though with each sucessive thrilling dash / it heaves up huge between my thighs / this hot and heaving sweating beast / it tugs my hips / it heaves me on / on to the golden hills of Acheron / I grip him hard / my knees dig in I soar up high / I float / I flow / I'm thrown into the sky and then thud down / the air is singed in smells of mud / crushed grass / horse shit and sweat / mixed up in one divine and bloody mess / we've lorst the fucker / oh bloody balls the nag's confused / the scent is lorst / the dogs go searching / now confused / now whining / now all cross / oh shit and piss! The fucking league of love the bloody foxes sabotaged the scent! / The careful thread, the ribbon of fear that leads us on to the bloody kill / those left-wing bastards jealous as hell / to see their betters enjoying themselves / threw scent to confuse / those rotten sods / I'd thrash them black and blue I'd have them flogged / those dirty, poofy, marxist, working class yobs / wait! Pluto's found the scent again! Oh fab. We're off! Tarquin bloodies one of their noses! Oh heavens, it's just raining roses / he's on the ground and Tarquin's ready to drive his horse into the bugger / Jeremy says nay / restrains hot Tarquin / they'll come another day! He says / oh bravo! Dashing! Super! Wow! I'm going now / look at meeeeeee! / The days's spun rich in magenta to auburn / the hounds shriek louder / the scent grows strong / the fox is tired / my cheeks are red / my eyes are bright / blood will be shed / oh god it's getting fucking awful thrilling / the flesh *is* weak but the spirit is willing / my pants have come galore / and my ass is deliciously bloody sore / we're close / the fox has gone to ground / we'll find the little beastly hound / yes! It's trapped down in some gully / horses crash through the farmer's land / all in a hurry / tear up the crops / oh dear / we'll pay later never fear / oh fuck! Some kid's pet cat is torn to shreds in the wake of the enthusiastic chase / never mind there's plenty more / ah, we've got him now / I see it caught / it's trapped / its breath is pounding out in horrible short stabs / its fear setting each hair on end / the hounds all teeth and smiles as they go in and sink their fangs into its throat / the blood was one long jet / just fabulous / I'm sure the fox was pleased to make his end this way / the fury / the chase / the ecstasy / the embrace / the leader dismounts / cuts off its tail / bloodies the kids / oh they were thrilled / oh what a day / let's have a gin and tonic / whadya say / lovely life / wouldn't have it any other way /

STEVE.   I must say you've made me thirsty / let's have a drink o.k. / I enjoyed that / shame about the cat.

HELEN.   Ice?

STEVE.   Masses *(she mimes handing him the glass)* I like getting pissed / like the sound / the crisp crunched feel of bursting ice / crushed diamonds melting in the acid of your vice / I'll have a tequila / a frozen glass / grind it into a salt sea bath / squeezed lemon sharp as a razor / as a spinster's tongue, a gob of cointreau adds the dash of fun shake it hard then pour it out / into your icy salt-licked glass / the first tastes nice and bitter sweet / grips the tip of your tongue / like the mouth of a baby on a mother's teat / well have another / that chases through / warms the furnace / rattles a window or two / the third one slides along the avenue / well lined by now and gets to work / a glow appears / your inhibitions crumble and your fears, they take a gentle tumble / number four drags from the cupboard your other self / the Jekyll to your Hyde / watch yourself bloom as four pours blood into the withered you. No. five / proves the fact that you're alive after all / and not a dreary fucking bore / it knocks on other doors down deep / out come the demons from their wretched sleep / so pleased at last to be set free / let's have some fun he! he! he! here comes your past / persecution mania opens his door / the alcohol prises open a few more / paranoia, guilt / jealousy and hate / ready to rehearse the message of agro and bile / you feel good / number six adds fuel to the fire / there's a party down there raging within / your best friend now you hate worse than sin / you and you / piss off you splat / I don't give a shit / accuse and slag / it's all coming out now / like an acid bath / it unpeels the old varnish / removes the old scabs / the wounds now feel fresh, alive and they sting / I throw down number seven / gis another I sing / insults are woken from some ancient time / spit out again / some antediluvian forgotten crime / but I wanna 'nother / I'm having a great time / I'm dragging out the dirty linen and all the grimes / and too much / it dampens the fire / rather than blaze / the one over the edge / the door slams shut in your brain / the demons return to their old domain / pandora's box is shut again / you grab another in the hope that you can entice rather than drown but all you've got is slush and sentiment / tears in the eye and howl! Forgive me darling / I didn't mean it / you cry / the party's over / you're left with the mess and your pain / old news-papers lashed by rain / fuck it, I wanna 'nother drink / you've had nine! I don't care no more / it's my second wind / I feel fine / shit it's good / but as the sunset scorches a blazing exit from the skies and just as quickly lays down and dies / so my good feeling pissed off just as fast and left me with an empty glass / gimme — I slurp my number ten / it's late / the light snaps off inside your skull / darkness falls / I feel like hell / and then the next thing then you will espy is the lav staring you in the eye / up come your guts / lurch / past, acids through in one hot stinking steaming stew / your mouth a cesspit of rot-ting food / it reeks, like shit flows out your head / you just can't wait to get inside your bed.

HELEN.   If that's a good time / I'd rather be dead!

Fade out.

Scene Eight

Scene appears with SYBIL *and* LES *on top of her: same dialogue to begin it as earlier scene.*

LES.   Was that all right for you?

SYBIL.   Yeah — it was great. Was it all right for you?

LES.   Yeah . . . lovely . . . do you enjoy it?

SYBIL.   Yeah . . . it was . . . nice . . . did you?

LES.   Wo?

SYBIL.   Enjoy it!

LES.   Yeah — it was handsome!

SYBIL.   So with all the thrills and all the spills in the end you're over the hill / you are no further, no, in the exploit than when I first discovered my painful plight / you shift your plates of meat from side to side, plan murder, death, cyanide. But in the end we watch TV and larf at arse holes making mugs of all our class / you sit / swill down a jug of gin / play with your balls / say 'ark at him'! Football and darts, the mind boggles at the space that runs between your ears / the working classes ruled always by their peers / 'cause daft you are and thick / that's why you live like pigs / she, chained to a sink / and my old man / that pontz! you can't face with your empty bontz / 'cause you're afraid — his accent frightens you away /

LES.   Don't make me laugh / do me a turn / fink his dialogue will make me squirm / fink a chatter with his nibs will set old Les a-trembling on his pegs / 'cause he can utter 'olesome tones. It's content, what goes in to make his bones / it's there the marrow mate! F. off you stupid come-pot. Slag stained hag / you filthy load of ancient slag / why should I enunciate to him the dirty fink I hate / it's him that I'll annihilate / without the chatter / with no threat of tongue wobble banter / like two poofs ready to tear each others' wigs off. No screaming heebie geebies no! When I k'blast him / watch me go!

SYBIL.   Yeah tell me another / six months it's been my Les / you can't make up your mind / like Hamlet in a tizz / you come all over heavy like a patton tank / but when it comes to deeds / your chat is merely wanks / you've lost me Les / I'll find some geyser new / who will do for me what I do do for you / some hard determined lad that will not me disgrace / not lay a single finger on his rotten face! / not volunteer a bunch of fives to show him your love's alive / let alone / the murder, death and dark revenge you swore / when you were in my minge / once there you would swear all / and like the famous rat / that in escaping from the claws of some fat cat / falls in a vat of wine / cries out, 'save me! Save me cat! I'd rather be eaten alive than drown, oh horror in that vat of wine.' The cat concurs and flips the rat out on his paws / whereupon seeing himself on steady floors, rat scarpers to safe hole inside the wall. The cat now flaming mad to see he's been so badly had says 'you said I could eat you rat if I plucked you from out that vat' to which the rat replied . . . 'you'll say anything when you're drunk' / that's you all right you punk!

LES.   What a turnabout / what a double choke to suffer slagging from the slut I poke / you think I am not waiting, choosing well before consigning adenoids to hell / don't make me piss my pants / don't make me laugh / death takes its time / it stalks a lonely path. Conditions must be good / the hour right / don't mess it up and make me rush it / right! I'll have him sure, I swear I will / but do it all careful like / now — here's the spiel / I got a plan / now listen to your desperate dan. I'll destroy him with **telepathy!** By my magic powers I turn on the heat / I concentrate with all my strength / tune into his wave length and crumble goes his brain's network, cells and nerve centres go berserk / like radios jamming enemies' airwaves / my mind will send him in a rave / he'll freak, twitch and explode when senses he my vicious probes. I read it in a book how you can work the spell or spook some geyser into living hell / by concentration / thinking on his boat / or staring hard at his mug that's in a phot / fix on his eyes and pour a thousand evil thoughts inside / he'll cop the message every night like needles in his brain and burning bright / 'til sickness claim him like a bride / — so much cleaner than cyanide /

SYBIL.   Where do you cop that pile of shit / I fink he's doing it to you, you twit.

Scene Nine

STEVE *and* HELEN.

STEVE.   Cigarette?

HELEN.   Thanks darling. Nearly killed someone with my car last night.

STEVE.   Oh really darling. Were you pissed?

HELEN.   Couldn't see the bugger.

STEVE.   Oh, why was that?

HELEN.   He was so damn black

STEVE.   Couldn't you see the whites of his eyes?

HELEN.   His back was towards me

STEVE.   I hate the bastards. No no no no no. I won't say that / just find them different to us / white is white and brown is brown and black is black / you know what I mean? / they're fabulous, in their place / in Jamaica I found them just ace / a gas / great sense of humour / and move like a dream / they're all instinct is what I mean / whereas we think / to create and rule / they feel all the time / like children and play with their tools / they want before their time / they want the taste of power / but their minds are no higher than their stomachs / even lower / my god what do they put in the shit that they gobble / I can't imagine / it makes my knees just wobble / You can't give in to the kaffir / to the wog / just because they demand it / my god, what would they do to us / they must be trained not to rebel / but to use their brain as well / if we gave in to every tin pot black / they'd be throwing spears and hurling threats / even atomic bombs / yes! / It could come to that / they're thick / good natured / more like a dream / but don't feel pain / not like us is what I mean / they're tough / more like the animals / they kill and chop each other up / life's not worth a fig / a string of beads and they'd sell their mum / of course we're all brothers under the sun / but I hate my fucking brother even if we've got the same mum / don't persecute the fuckers / they're all right blokes / there's one down at the club / he takes in the coats / don't kill or hurt them / just put them on the bloody boats / please Maggie put your money where your mouth is / don't be all talk and no fuck / stick up for us — have a little pluck. My god she's a handsome woman / I bet the man who gets inside her pants has a lot to answer for / oh don't look at me like that / we're all the same / there's not a man in England who wouldn't drop his Y fronts for that dame / still look at the unemployment and sponging in the name of socialism / half of them are on the game / could you touch one love / I mean could you / it's rumoured that they're hung like bloody mules / well it's not such a rumour actually / one day at the club they let in one / the laws that make us do these things / so anyway, in the shower I caught a glimpse of the bugger / I just couldn't believe it darling *(mimes)* it was simply obscene / it made me feel like a shrimp and you know I'm quite well endowed

HELEN *(fast)*. Yes yes darling, of course

STEVE.   He should have it covered up or at least require a yearly licence for it / so I threw down my card at the club office and said / shove that up your jack if you let in any more of that / he's the Prince of Morocco they replied / oh well, I said, that puts a different complexion on the face / of course they have to travel / our royals do it for the trade / they have to shake hands even eat with the bloody spades / they do it for the cash / the foreign office tells them to / you wouldn't catch them with the buggers otherwise / not after work / not in the house / why — they wouldn't get past the dogs / who have never seen one in the house / wouldn't know a bloody wog / what! we must preserve what's English / or British if you must, though it's very hard to think of paddy quite like us / there is no place like England / you can't sing there'll always be a Great Britain / it doesn't have the taste / or there'll always be an England . . .

Sings, and HELEN *accompanies. They get through two verses.*

Sorry darling, it brings a tear to my old face whenever I hear that good refrain / let's keep it clean love / let's keep it white / kick out the packies, blackies, paddys and kikes / go back to the jungle / Belfast and Israel / don't turn our happy haven into a rancid hell.

Scene Ten

HELEN.   We mustn't be late, you mustn't dip your spoon into the cup of hate / it's the first night / the audience will be sheer delight, and I assure you, they will be absolutely white! I'll wear something stunning / I'll just astound / the important thing darling is to make you proud *(she mimes the following)* I'll wear a fulsome daring Chanel robe / slashed to the thigh / in black cashmere / gathered from the bellies of baby goats / it hugs every line every detail made clear / every vale of my body / every genital contour will amplify itself on my exterior / arms gathered and arranged in gossamer ripples that float in waves / belt by Fiorucci from the skin of snakes that slither round glistening lakes / the gown weighted down at the hem which flares allowing a flash of golden thigh as I climb the stairs / so demure on the outside / such a whore within / fashion is so divine it makes dressing up a sin / a rash display of silver filigree curls round my cheeks / and makes my bum two silver moons that I display for fun / the gown now draws my flesh down from those swelling curves tapering at the thigh / then up it rushes scooping my tits like tasty cherry pies / they softly float inside their silken net like two blancmanges wanting to be ate / a pair of shoes in satin with five inch heels forged from venetian glass / opaque and hollow / here small glow worms shine in the dark / my stockings must be silk and finish at the thigh / tops grasped by black suspender belt / like lizards teeth held tight / my knickers, sheer opaque and thin made from crushed water silk / within, the gussett tiny pleats will hold my special midnight treats / soft and crushy / nice and sweet / my hair is gathered up in waves / is spun and twisted into furls / is plaited, combed and arranged in precious curls / it's modelled on Utrillo's nymph rising from the sea /

Sassoon spent many sleepless nights creating this dream for me / my arms, my love will be as long white snakes beneath transparent tulle / sewn in with chrysoprases and tiny pearls / I'm ready now darling / let's swirl /

Opera music comes on, STEVE *mimes eating chocolates with* HELEN, *opera concludes, grand applause which turns into* LES *and* SYBIL *slagging each other which then turns back to* STEVE *and* HELEN *applauding once more.*

STEVE. Then after the opera

HELEN. The supper

STEVE. Is it at the Savoy?

HELEN. Is it Rules?

STEVE. Kettners is now a hamburger joint

HELEN. The Caprice is over too

STEVE. We'll go to The Zanzibar, that will do.

HELEN. My lover holds out my coat / my wrap of pink ermine / he opens the door / the air smells like wine / that special time when the evening is yours / gone to bed are the swine / outside, the porter / the cab is hailed /

STEVE. Taxi!

HELEN. The air crisp and tangy / my lover in tails / expectancy hangs like some fine perfume / he squeezes my shoulder / he says

STEVE. How are you?

HELEN. I'm lovely darling I must reply / we watch the big red buses go sludging by / heaving their cargoes of workers and aged.

STEVE. Here's our cab darling.

HELEN. The porter is paid

STEVE. Great Queen Street please *(they get in taxi)* Cigarette?

HELEN. Thank you my sweet / my hands find your prick / I feel somewhat shy / as cabby in mirror steals sneaky spy the world is closed to us / wrapped in our love and wealth / I snuggle up close / your coat is rough / you feel manly and tough / and smell of Musk / your shiny powdered chin and brilliant teeth / you're a blade all right / you make me weak at the knees / you sparkle / you thunder / your hat sits just right / a trilby snapped brim / a Bogart or a Flynn / I like my man tough / I like to be ruled by an iron fist but a velvet tool within / I love you opening the doors and getting the bills / make yourself broke indulging my sins / being the master / ruling me / a genius in bed / an expert driving me crazy / weak as a kitten up a tree / let me wait for your call / let me pine / let me fret / and when the phone rings / my heart goes pitta-pat / send me an orchid ply me with perfume / from Givenchy, Chanel and Cardin as well / say how pretty you look tonight / say how swell / I can't have enough of that / grab my elbow / squeeze it tight / guide me darling into the light / like I was helpless / without my sight / let me blaze like a meteor shower / you make me feel good / you have the power / I gleam for you / I sparkle / I'll effervesce display me like a proud conquest / like a trophy like an animal from the jungle tamed / wild cat to others / for you love a lamb / you'll be proud / you'll look suave in your black and white / you devil from hell / you lucifer / anti-christ / you hypnotize me with your blazing eyes / your adamantine personality / let's go lover / oh! I must have a pee!

Scene Eleven

STEVE.   We escape to the restaurant / at last some repose / throw off your coat darling / powder your nose / put on some lip gloss / I'll splash my toes / hello Giovanni / 'How is M'sieur and Madame tonight?' / his bright teeth assure us that all is quite normal and right / all is quite safe / the window's double barred / 'gainst the dreaded I.R.A. / our table is ready / how simply hooray / elated wide-eyed / we view the sight / a river of Lords, Barons and Knights / a stream of gold, diamonds and pearls / a torrent of lawyers, judges and Earls / a splatter of royalty on top / *(aside)* (hallo Charles, hallo Di) just the sauce that lends a perfect flavour to all / a small royal sprinkling seems to draw from the rest a flavour that's absolutely the best / Aperitif? Cinzano and bitterlemon / a crunch of ice / it tastes like heaven / What would Monsieur and Madame like? Some salmon fumé / smoked just perfect / its flesh tears like silk / was spawned in scotch lakes / hung to be cured by those that know the secret of salmon / the ones with the nose / to follow avocado stuffed with prawns / garlic to taste / crushed in a paste / pear as soft as the bellies of babes / prawns crisp as ice / champagne perignon washes all away in its tide / the mashed hors d'oeuvres / all's clean inside / the mouth is pink and raw once again / to receive like gargantua its morsels of fun / what now, oh love decide / steak au poivre or le boeuf sur le toit, noisette d'agneau or poached turbot / crab freshly dropped in a boiling scream so its flesh is sunset pink and taste a dream / filet mignon with oysters crushed with sauces / that sounds a must / we'll have two of those / some escargots on the side / they taste so divine / cooked in sweet herbs and wine / a Mouton Rothschild chilled to a thaw / wash it down / hmm! Delicious / let's have some more / I slice the steak / its blood runs free / raw as a wound / soft as a kiss / I embrace it / I swallow the last ecstatic piece / it flows like lava into me / a mountain of spinach and acre of mushroom / we shove it all in and still there's room / more champagne! It showers away the fish and the garlic / the slightly acid taste / the burp, the silver of nausea that starts to grow / from compound of prawns, salmon, beef, oysters, the sparkly flows / we're fresh again darling / order / what did you say? More champagne / my god you're stacking it away / more champagne / dry cold and wild / what — you've got no more Mouton Rothschild / well, give us the best, the best that you've got / get fucking moving you Italian git / no, sorry! What did I say? I was joking, what / you're my friend / *(aside)* fucking waiter pretending he's the bloody end / just 'cause he had Charlie and Diana to dine / he thinks his piss now tastes like wine / yes, we'll have some cheese / we'll have some armontal, gruyere, fine herbs and some brie / it must be dead ripe / it must ooze gently / just enough / no more / if it's runny I'll hurl your fucking cheese through the door / I'm joking you cunt / now don't get sore / more champagne / I said more / now caviar to finish / taken at the end it's perfect when you think you can't shove more in your head / a spoonful of caviar will slither around and find a space there you hadn't found / more champagne darling? / Feeling all right? Yes! Crêpe suzette / brandy éclairs / rum babas and liqueur pears / hmm! That's gurgly / that's rich and oozy / god it squelches past / my guts are on fire / more champagne I gasp / I can hardly breathe / give me a cigar / a brandy / something that doesn't take the remotest inch of any more space / I couldn't bear to think there's any more space left / the remotest chink that might house some morsel / some unexplored delight / that might put the cap on the perfect night / so now I feel fine / I need a shit / oh shit, I can't move / I want to be sick / I want to heave up / be back in a tick / I'll shit and I'll piss and I'll blow the house down / Ha! Ha! Ha! Oh fuck it's coming up / can you sick, shit and piss all at once? It must be a record / see you darling / sorry I'm such a sight /

HELEN.   Darling, don't apologise / it's been a wonderful night!

Scene Twelve

LES.   It's no good / this geyser's got me by the balls / can't seem to work my little plan / I'm not really a desperate man or dan / so what he's off with his high class dame / so what, for them life's just a game / not like us / working for our bread / get up / alarm clock near our bed / a bunk up when we're not too tired from slog / hustling down the highest. For the cheapest flog / can we afford the trip this year / we're overdrawn / oh fuck / the kids need more socks / look what they took for tax this week love / no meat today, we'll look for scraps / they make a lovely soup / o.k. / petrol's up and smokes are dear / it's much cheaper to be a ginger beer these days it really is / 'cause there's no hope / no none with kids / in the pub / kicked out at time / 'let's have your glasses / there's always tomorrow' / but not for them with clubs / and out all night 'cause they don't have to graft at break of light / they can lay abed 'til ten / have coffee rolls sent in to them / fiddle / screw the state / form companies and liquidate / they do it legal like, like all of them / but if we do a straight thieve they shove us in the pen / at least our thieving's honest / break and enter / armed robbery / a good old fashioned thieve / but those bastards do it legally / lawyers, companies, minutes and fraud / and end up in the House of Lords / she's right / whenever I hear his voice I go weak at the knees / it's not from choice / it's something ingrown like a toenail / the neverhads have always doffed their hats to those wot have / it's the voice / the style / the polite smile / with millions at their beck and call / they can still hold us in thrall / it's like a pyramid / us at the base / pile of stupid trash / fed by all that's worst in life / Daily Mirror / football, Wimpy bars and darts / to make sure the workers stay working class / artless pile of muck / fit only for a piss up and Fray Bentos heated up when we get in / and keep your noses down /

here's the boss / here's the police / here's the judge / here's the royals / ooh! ain't she sweet / what dress will she wear this week / brain-washed workers waving flags at coronation dressed in rags / the cost of war is going up / the bear is on the move again / I do not wish to fight and kill to satisfy some other pervert's will / when if I take my vengeance private like / I get ten years / but do it wholesale / killa lot in uniform to make it legal / they pin a medal and make it regal / so my hate's not hot enough / to shove a knife in this pontz's guts / I'll let him fade out like the dinosaur / and kick out this bitch my whore.

Scene Thirteen

SYBIL.   Coward like all his kind / why should I fucking care / when men are two a penny fuck him / snap my fingers, I'll find some more / they're sitting ducks / all they want to do is . . . need I say it twice / they're all so easy such a bore / a bit of titillation and they're yours / a hard-on makes him soppy as a kid / drooling for his candy / they think of nothing else, and when they're randy / why, it's like taking from a kid his candy / we fuck the bastards / but not quick / just trap them with a tender kiss / suss out the guy and check his bankability / his standing in the world / be careful dear / don't cast your pearls before bankrupt swine / don't fuck for love for fuck's sake / cast your net and wag your tail / they'll soon be slobbering for you / never fails / the child / man heroes think they claim you as pussy hovers in their dreams / dash that image / or you're just a dustbin for his passion's lust / receptacle for spunk / give him a taste and then withdraw a while / he'll crave for more and more / think your pussy's made of gold and myrrh / he'll write poems to your asshole the pathetic cur / tantalise / don't be too keen / like dope pushers, give the first lot free / hook him first with your sweet sting / then play the game / don't be around when hard-on rings / so then the drug has bit / you're in his blood you won't be so damn free the next time / let him crawl, he'll think you're just the end / you'll be Nirvana / a goddess, Aphrodite, perfect divine and rare / to what my love shall I compare thy hair / he'll think he's Shakespeare and go fucking spare / since he thinks that he's found grace / the perfect elusive face / then let him back / be sweet and let the cunt relax once more / even be his little whore / then whack! withdraw!! 'You don't love me any more'. He's hanging on just by his nails / just be unsure / 'I don't know if we're right my dear' / make him grovel, sleepless nights / this bit is very tricky girls and risky too / he may decide he's better without **you** / if he's got strength / one ounce too much / you may lose him and start at square one all again / but chances are, like Pavlov's dogs, the jerks confused / you now seem, if it works / immortal to the Burke / you're gold dust, opium, exotic fruit / he's on his knees then kick him in the teeth / then hold on fast / he's weak / go for the dough / a wife comes next / then in for the kill / house, pro- tection and at last his will / and not the one he leaves / the one that keeps his brains in place / dislodge that and you're made / dangle him a while then snuggle up / be his sweet bride / and then he thinks **he's** conquered in the world the only one that fate for him has squired / he's proud / it's been a chase / an easy game not so laced in danger with that smell of fame / reputation goes up / high class dame / to trap an animal cunning is necessary but if you trap a lion it's more tough / the going's hard and lonely, but on your wall he makes a smashing trophy / but then it's all the same / beast and human man / they're just big game / you do not get them by being nice / you get them by cunning skill and shrewd device / or else be sweet and honest girl and be well fucked, four kids and end in hell / liberation?? This is it girl!

Scene Fourteen

They come together for the final dance.

STEVE.   I like to dance.

HELEN.   I like tea in the Ritz.

STEVE.   I like to fly / sipping champagne in the sky.

HELEN.   I like to wriggle my hips to the beat in my heart / turn and twist.

STEVE.   I like to Fred Astaire and Jean Kelly / I like to lick absinth off your belly.

HELEN.   I like to smell like a wild garden after rain.

STEVE.   I like the pleasure I derive after pain. I like holding your waist seeing red rubies glance off your face.

HELEN.   Dance under stardust whirling in the sky.

STEVE.   Glittering lights / diamonds shattering your eye.

HELEN.   Violets, thick carpets and cocktails.

STEVE.   Invitations on embossed cards / to rub shoulders with the rich and special.

HELEN.   Long fingers bejewelled with art nouveau.

STEVE.   Like fireworks burning bright.

HELEN.   Pearls and amathysts crushed in white. I like to wake with the sea licking my ears cocooned in silken sheets / my dreams dissolving in the morning dawn so sweet.

STEVE.   Like butter melting over hot meat / your ass as round as warm doughnuts.

HELEN.   Your cock sliced between my bum.

STEVE.   Like a hot dog nestled in a bun / your hair like a soft meadow over the lacy white pillow.

HELEN.   The soft knock on the door.

STEVE. The coffee and rolls and first steaming piss.

HELEN. The shower and broiling in a mist.

STEVE. The morning papers white and crisp. Murders and rape . . .

HELEN. Taken with cheese and grapes . . .

STEVE. Stabbings and bombs . . .

HELEN. More coffee my love . . .

STEVE. Earthquakes and deaths . . .

HELEN. Toast and poached eggs . . .

STEVE. Starvation and famine . . .

HELEN. Sausages and Gammon.

STEVE. You arise like Venus striding out of the skies.

HELEN. We leave the murder and crime in crunched newspapers never to begrime the spotless lives that are yours and mine.

STEVE. They belong in the other place where people walk in arsenic and hate.

HELEN. Where envy follows greed and becomes the seed that seeks to flower in our pot.

STEVE. No hope of that / we're protected at the top / from our exalted eyrie we float like eagles over the predators below.

HELEN. Who do the pools or any other hype that cons your greedy minds that you may be the one that fortune finds.

STEVE. When the chances are greater that you'll be killed than achieve your fortune by fates will.

HELEN. So in your beehive metropolis you breath and hope.

STEVE. Turn on the telly.

HELEN. And go to bed when the weather forecast is read.

STEVE. Your eyes will squint and grow crows feet staring at the fine print and the lowest price.

HELEN. We have no thought of cost damn it but only what is nice.

STEVE. Your eyes my darling will only read the make and no price tag will ever forbid you to take.

HELEN. You will never arise.

STEVE. No never surmise a better life as long as beer doesn't rise by more than two pence a pint.

HELEN. You'll be alright Jack.

STEVE. Let's go darling it's getting light.

HELEN. Let's watch the dawn arise in its vast magic palace of light.

STEVE.   Thanks Giovanni, it's been a wonderful night. Cigarette? . . .

They both light cigarettes and inhale deeply and as the light fades they age in the results of their debauched lives.

Greek

Greek was first performed at the Half Moon Theatre, London, on 11 February, 1980. The cast was as follows:

EDDY and FORTUNE-TELLER	Barry Philips
DAD and MANAGER OF CAPE	Matthew Scurfield
WIFE, DOREEN, and WAITRESS 1	Linda Marlowe
MUM, SPHINX, and WAITRESS 2	Janet Amsden

Directed by Steven Berkoff

Greek was transferred to the Arts Theatre Club, London, in September 1980. The cast was as follows:

EDDY and FORTUNE-TELLER	Barry Philips
DAD and MANAGER OF CAFE	Matthew Scurfield
WIFE, DOREEN, and WAITRESS 1	Linda Marlowe
MUM, SPHINX, and WAITRESS 2	Deirdre Morris

Directed by Steven Berkoff

Place: England

Time: present

Stage setting: kitchen table and four simple chairs. These will function in a number of ways. They can be everything one wants them to be from the platform for the SPHINX to the café. They also function as the train; the environment which suggests EDDY's humble origins becoming his expensive and elaborate home in Act Two. The table and chairs merely define spaces and act as an anchor or base for the actors to spring from. All other artifacts are mimed or suggested. The walls are three square upright white panels, very clinical and at the same time indicating Greek classicism. The faces are painted white and are clearly defined. Movement should be sharp and dynamic, exaggerated and sometimes bearing the quality of seaside cartoons.

ACT ONE

Scene One

EDDY. So I was spawned in a Tufnell Park that's no more than a stone's throw
from the Angel / a monkey's fart from Tottenham or a bolt of phlegm from
Stamford Hill / it's a cess pit, right . . . a scum hole dense with the drabs who
prop up corner pubs, the kind of pub where ye old ass holes assemble . . . the
boring turds who save for Xmas with clubs . . . my mum did that . . . save all
year for her slaggy Xmas party of boozy old relatives in Marx and Sparks'
cardigans who stand all year doing as little as they can while they had one
hand in the boss's till and the other scratching their balls . . . they'd all come
over and vomit up guinness and mum's unspeakable excuse for cuisine all
over the bathroom, adjust their dentures . . . rage against the blacks, envying
their cocks, loathe the yids envying their gelt . . . hate everything that walks
under thirty and fall asleep in front of the telly . . . so they'd gather in the pubs,
usually a smelly corner pub run by a rancid thick as pig shit paddy who sold
nothing but booze and crisps in various chemical flavours to their yokel
patrons who played incessant games of cruddy darts, drink yards of stale
gnat's piss beer and chatter like, 'see Arsenal last week . . . I think England's
team's all washed up . . . what abaht the was he dribbled the . . . nah nah, he's
lorst his bottle . . . do leave orf . . .' the stink of the pub rises and the OAPs sit
in the corner staring out into the dreams they never had with a drip of snot
hanging off the ends of their noses and try to make a pint last four hours . . .
start crowding up now and the paddy starts raving fucking time and pulling
the glass out of your hand while he's bursting your eardrums screaming like a
sergeant major his wife attempts to shovel some paint on her evil hate-all face
which looks as if it's been applied by a drunken epileptic on a roller
coaster . . . 'allo luv', she foams . . . staring out of a yellow face with little snot
brown eyes like two raisins in a plate of porridge. And if by chance you lean
over the bar too far some bastard monster cunt alsatian leaps at you, its dripping fangs simply dying to rip your fucking throat out . . . so I gave up going to
the corner pub with its late night chorus of lurchy 'g'nights and see ya Tell'' we
got wine bars now, handsome.

That's much better — sit down, a half bottle of château or bollinger, some
paté and salad served by a chick who looks as if she's been fresh frozen . . .
you take your favourite woman there, my woman, very nice mate, looks like

she's been just minted and sharp as new mown grass, knickers as white as Xmas, eyes like the bluest diamonds / a pair of fiery red rubies for lips, the light hits them and shatters your eyes, she smiles and your heart leaps into your throat and you carry a demon between your thighs and up to your chin / the whole time . . . I wear shades to protect myself against the brightness of her teeth . . . no tobacco stains on them boy . . . breath like an ocean breeze on Brighton Pier . . . now could you take her to that pub? Could you ever! Nah! It's really for the old fascists singing war songs on the pavement and knees up mother Brown. So I go to my wine bar with my bird who's carved out of onyx and marble and laced in the smells of the promise of sex the way you wouldn't believe . . . I swim in her like I was plunging into the Jordan for a baptism. So anyway one day my dad calls me in the kitchen. Come in son, he says, I wanna chat to ya, or we could go down the corner to the pub, I'll buy you a drink. No! not that pub I yelp in real and unfeigned terror. I'll throw some tea into a pot instead . . . mums out . . . the Daily Mirror crossword half finished . . . well it is a bit grotty but homely in a sickly sort of way if you're not used to anything better it's not like the interior of a zen temple but cosy. A few crumbs on the carpet, some evil photos of my sister on the mantelpiece and a picture of granny looking like Mussolini in drag which they all looked like in those far off days of pre-history, the poodles shit again behind the cocktail cabinet . . . the old bacon rinds sit stinking in the pan and the room renches of lard. I made dad a cuppa. Mum's at bingo and sis' is meditating in the bedroom on the squeezing out of some juicy blackheads . . . her old knickers lie sunny side up . . . she always left them on the floor for mum to scoop up while I wouldn't have touched them except with those pincers that pick up radium behind thick walls. So we sit down and he confesses this story to me . . . pulls out a fag and sits there with his flies half undone, and the ash of his fag ready to drop all over his shirt. I try not to look at him or his flies. I try to occupy my thoughts with my latest Stan Kenton. I look out of the window and see the grey clouds of Tottenham stray across the window pane . . . a tiny sliver of sun is struggling to peep through sees what it has to shine on and thinks 'fuck it — is it worth it' and beats a retreat. So dad says 'look here son' I says 'yes, dad' clocking his work-raped face, his tasteless shit heap Burton ready made trousers and his deadly drip dry shirt that acquires BO faster than shit attracts flies . . . I clock all this fusion of rubbish and say 'yes dad? what do you want to chat abaht', never hearing much else out of his gob than 'send the darkies back to the jungle' and 'Hitler got the trains running on time' . . . you got a lot of nazi lovers among the British down and out. Lazy bastards wondered why at the end of a life of skiving and strikes Moisha down the road copped a few bob or why the Cypriots had a big store full of goodies not that pathetic shit heap down our street that flogs only mothers pride mousetrap cheese a few miserable tins of pilchards and Heinz baked beans and a dreary cunt inside saying, 'no we don't get no demand for that' when asked for something only slightly more exotic than Kelloggs. So dad did not come out with any of that fascist bullshit which relieved me since the Front were full of dads like this and that cunt in the grocery shop . . . 'yeah dad' I said 'what's on your bonce' . . . his face squeezed up like it's hard to say, like those old ads for Idris lemon squash showing a screwed up lemon and comes out with . . .

Scene Two

DAD.   When you were a nipper / we went to a gypsy, a fortune teller / bit of a
giggle / an easter fair / don't laugh / a caper what else / spent a tosheroon on
a bit of a thrill don't talk to me about thrills / so in we went / the gypsy asks
'have I a son?' 'I have' I says, I mean who don't have a son? His face meanwhile staring into the ball / his eyes all popping / I'm not taking it for gen,
straight up a lark / easter and all / I've got a lovely bunch and all that / his face
gets all contorted and twisted and he says / he sees a violent death for this
son's father / do what! but I'm his dad / come orf it / don't get all dramatic /
we get on like houses blazing / and I see he says, something worse than death
/ and that's a bunk-up with his mum / I'll give you a backhand I utter / you're
having me on / you been smoking them African woodbines / no he shrieks I
see it, and what I see I see / so don't pay me, just scarper / leave my tent /
keep your gelt / outside we ran, your mum was white as Persil / I as yellow as
a chinaman with jaundice / course we took no notice / forgot about it like,
but not quite / waited till you got to be a bloke and then one day I said Dinah /
you remember that darkie in the fair who came out with all that filth about
Eddy, one morning in bed just lying there, redigesting bits of past and sucking
still the flavour of some juicy memories . . . 'not many' our Dinah slurps . . .
'not many, I nearly dropped Doreen with whom I was six months pregnant
then / funny times' . . . well I say, that fair is back in town, the same firm fif-
teen years later . . . let's bowl down and see that geezer, tell that Hornsey
gypsy what a lot of old bollocks / how he upset my missus with his pack of
dirty lies / so off we went / doubted somehow that he'd still be there, since he
was pushing 60 then / you never know, we waited our turn / it was the same
name "have your future read / Fantoni's magic crystal gazer" . . . shall we go
in? . . .

MUM.   . . . do you think we should? . . .

DAD.   Why not, it's now or never / we went pale a bit but in we marched /
same old schmutter on the table, the beads we walked through and the bit of
old glass and no, it weren't him, so I said where's the old geezer that we once
saw whose handle now you seem to have / 'my late old man' / he said / 'five
years ago he uttered his last / and fell off the perch / but taught me the trade /
imbued his vision in me / I got his powers now / so don't you fret / if he did
good by you / donate a quid and I'll do my best' / . . . so Ed, your mum and I
sat down just like before / the years they shrank away / just like a hole fell out
the earth and time and space had faded away / we seemed then to have hur-
tled back those 15 years / in that small tent / the music tinkling through from
the carousel outside and that funny smell / the shouts growing faint just the
whiff of stale grass under our feet / and like the tent seemed small / like a trap
and suddenly hot and nothing outside just quiet but his face / his face getting
all twisted up just like his dad / his mouth all white and tight like an earth-
quake was going on inside his nut and his lips were straining against it coming
out / Dinah sussed but natch we waited / don't tell me I said you see a son of
mine / his eyes looked up affirmed / no word just that look and his tight
mouth / like holding back something worse than vomit / 'and you see something worse', I says, 'like a nasty accident perhaps' . . . He nodded, parted

his lips enough to mouth the word death which he hadn't the guts to sound. He then stared hard at Dinah / but we had enough and wanted not to hear the other half but fled / I turned and snatched the quid back from the table / don't know why / but like before when I got my money back / it seemed to say by taking back the gelt that it couldn't happen /his eyes looked like pity / like those sweet pics you get in Woollies of those kids with a tear just ripe to drop / I know it's just a fun fair Ed / a laugh, a bit of a giggle / I didn't blame the kid / what do you make of it son / you don't fancy your old mum do you son! you don't want to kill me do you boy.

DOREEN.   Leave off you two.

EDDY.   Doreen! His face hung there like a soggy worn out testicle / mouth open and eyes like carrier bags / fancy my mum! I could sooner go down on Hitler, than do anything my old man so gravely feared / no dad / but all this aggro and old wives tale gone and put you in a tiz / I'll leave home / split and scarper / the central line goes far these days and that's to foreign climes / I'll piss off tomorrow / I needed to escape this cruddy flat and this excuse seemed good as any / tata ma and pa. They waved to me outside the flats . . . my mum looked sad / her spotty apron wrapped round her like the flag of womanhood / I never saw her out of it / always standing in the kitchen like some darkie slave behind dad and me and sis . . .

DAD.   Bung us the toast

EDDY.   Where's the jam?

DOREEN.   Pig!

MUM.   More tea love?

DAD.   Bung us the toast

EDDY.   Where's the jam?

DOREEN.   Pig!

MUM.   More taters love?

DOREEN.   I'm on a diet

MUM.   More cake love?

EDDY.   No mum I've had six slices already

MUM.   Go on have some more

EDDY.   I don't want no more you rancid old boot

DAD.   Hey!

EDDY.   I'd spray affectionately

MUM.   Oh he don't like my cake

EDDY.   She'd simper . . . all right bung us another slice and I'll wedge it down wiv a mug of tea to slop it up a bit and she gazes at us with moist eyes on all of us slurping like fat pigs in a trough / we'd leave a wreck filled table, ma's washing up, how well she knew that washtop / dad's picking out losers in the worn out armchair — sis is fitting in her cap for the night's activity cussing and swearing   in   the   next   room   as   she   struggles   with   it . . .

DOREEN.   Fuck   it!

EDDY.   And mum sits in front of the box watching some dozy cretin making cunts out of the cunts who go on to win a few bob / mum's giggling in her glee / her legs like a patchwork quilt from hogging the electric fire, while I was in my little room plotting and dreaming of ruling the world / take a Charles Atlas course / wondering if the queen gets it often / or planning a dose of robbery wiv violets or glorious bodily charm / so in my little room I plotted smoked / played Stan Kenton and wanked wiv mums cooking oil. Now no more will I escape to my little domain . . . hearing the sounds of hughy phlegm in the next room through the snot encrusted walls. So all in a flash these thoughts slinked like maggots through my bonce as I waved my goodbyes to the fast diminishing figures of my mum and dad wed together in the distance like mould on cheese . . . my dad was the mould / never mad about him . . . as I reached the end of the road I could only see the apron and lost the figure / the apron stayed in my mind the longest. When my old lady went to the happy hunting ground I would frame that apron.

MUM.   Take good care of yourself

DAD.   Don't forget to write

DOREEN.   Got your photo

MUM.   Be a good boy

DAD.   Send us some money

DOREEN.   Miss yer

MUM.   Love yer Ed

DAD.   take care on the roads

DOREEN.   Au revoir

MUM.   Bye, boy . . .

Scene Three

DAD.   The toast is burnt

MUM.   Saw Vi the other day

DAD.   Neighbours don't complain no more

MUM.   Matilda's had six kittens

DAD.   Where's my smokes?

MUM.   'Ere, 'ave you seen the cooking oil?

DAD. I miss our little Ed

MUM. How will he fare strikes up and down the country

DAD. The City sits in a heap of shit

MUM. Of uncollected garbage everywhere

DAD. The heat waves turn it all to slime and filthy germs hang thickly in the air / the rats are on the march

MUM. Transport sits idly at the docks where workers slink around and for a hefty bribe may let you have your avocado or Dutch cabbage . . . petrol's obsolete as thousands of rusting cars lay swelling up our streets to vital services like ambulances which take a month to get from place to place

DAD. The country's in a state of plague / while parties of all shades battle for power to sort the shit from the shinola / the marxists and the worker's party call for violence to put an end to violence and likewise the wankers suggest hard solutions like thick chains and metal toecaps / Poisoned darts half inched from local taverns / anyone who wants to kill maim and destroy / arson, murder and hack are being recruited for the new revolutionary party / the fag libs are holding violent demos to be able to give head in the public park when the garbage strike is over and not to be persecuted for screwing on the top deck of buses

MUM. Fortes catering is resisting the staff's demand to be paid wages and is recruiting workers from the jungles of South America

DAD. Yet also strongly resisting the need to clear out the rats for which they are duly famous

MUM. Most of the stores are closed but Fortnums and Harrods soldier on shrilly packed with screaming advocates of limited nuclear drop on Hyde Park and so rid the country they say of a twisted bunch of rancid and perverted filth

DAD. The nights in Hyde Park are lit by fires and the sound of tom toms from the Brixton black workers revolutionary gay lib join forces with white is ugly forced abortion / wanking is not a town in China but an alternative to the filthy men female party group

MUM. Meanwhile the rats head down Edgware Road up to Oxford Street preparing to turn right into Bond Street / get down Piccadilly and raid Fortnums, pick up their mates at Fortes and join forces to make all resistance impossible seeing how all resistance is locked in internecine strife

DAD. The rats march across Piccadilly avoiding Soho where the food is dangerous even for rats, heading down to the Strand / collect the Savoy contingent, overfat rats not sleek for battle but just good germ carriers with rotten teeth head across Waterloo Bridge and the National Theatre . . . try to wake the theatre rats who have been long in coma from a deadly attack of nightly brainwash

MUM. Those that can be woken will begin the no. 2 division and streak up Drury Lane to Holborn and on to Kings Cross . . .

DAD. Avoiding the carcases of rotting football Scots swollen and putrefying on the streets / those who failed to make the train and died while waiting for the next one / their flesh is deadly / the rats come marching in

MUM. Maggot is our only hope love

DAD. If we only had more maggots to eat through the stinking woodpile. But how is poor Ed going to manage in all this? . . .

Scene Four

EDDY. The shit has hit the fan as if from a great height / I walked and walked / the sirens like wailing banshees from black marias tear along the garbage filled London streets, chock full of close shaved men in blue and clubs in black / stacked full of teeth hate-clenched / wiv fists all hungry for their daily exercise . . . the Scotties line the kerb face down in vomit which swishes down the rat-infested gutters . . . dumb jocks down for their dozy game of football / some excuse to flee their fat and shit-heap Marys in the tenements / they wear funny little hats with bobbles on and rotten teeth, they belch into the carbon air their rotgut fumes and sing a lurchy tune or two about owning some pox-ridden scab heap called Glasgow when they don't own a pot to piss in. Then one blue-eyed bobby lays a skull or five (well aimed, son) wide open. SMASH . . . SPLATTER . . . CLOBBER . . . take that you tartan git . . . CRASH . . . SHATTER . . . lovely . . . 'ere you, wot the fuck you doin' . . . shut up . . . KERACKKKK!!!!

The whores descend and drain their filthy wallets. With their con of fuck and as the jock steps inside for fantasies of London pussy. KERACK! a villain hard faced doth distribute a bit of sense with bars of iron / so on they go, the foul ignoble mob / they watch the match the wrong way round so pissed as newts and then they stagger into Euston station driven by a blind sense of instinct or smell to join their fellow tartans on their journey back. 'Ay 'ad a loovely taime'.

Meanwhile and spewing up the Mall down which I walked to escape the deadly gas from ten day haggis freshly heaved upon our silver London streets. When what do I espy but fuck and shit Macdougal and his paddies from Belfast and raring to blow up anything that moves. Thick eared with hands like bunches of bananas / their voices from afar were like a pack of baying hounds. They were an army dressd in blue serge suits and without exception pale blue eyes and liquid gelignite stuffed in their macs and little bombs in innocent sandwich bags . . . armpits concealing stinking sweaty guns ready to blow some mother's son's head off and spray the dusty Strand with thick rich ruby / knock off some chick who god forbid could be some sweet of mine / or take the legs off some poor cunt who happened to be hanging about / and then they get all stinking in their pubs and roar with leprechaunish glee . . . 'I've only got six guinnesses' . . . and fight to say who was the one to toss the bomb . . . 'whose round is it now? How many tommies did you spray apart? . . . my fucking husband's in the pub again' . . . How many boys were drowning in their blood / who that very night had kissed the loving girls fare-well . . . 'Jesus, Mary and Joseph' . . . How many mothers' daughters copped a face of shrapnel / lost an eye . . . 'Fuck my fucking husband, fuck it! . . .' How many mothers douse the graves of kids of 18 / wives and widows chat-ting to a piece of earth while you, you crock of gonorrhoea in serge wolf back another gallon, leer home to your Bridget alone and waiting with six kids and unwashed climb aboard dragging across her fleshy wastes your skimpy shred of dirty prick / poke it about a bit and come your drip of watery spunk 10 seconds later / she's lying there like a bloated cow / never known what coming is / only read about those soft explosions in the groin / heard rumours like / the only explosions paddy here can make are ones that make you scream in fucking agony and pain awash in blood not ecstasy and spunk. What a fucking obscenity that is . . . FUCK FUCK FUCK AND SHIT / MY FUCKING HUSBANDS LYING ACROSS THE ROAD / HIS LEGS ON ONE SIDE AND HIS TORSO ON THE OTHER. OH GOD HELP ME. OH MAGGOT SCRATCHER HANG THE CUNTS / HANG THEM SLOW AND LET ME TAKE A SKEWER AND JAB THEIR EYES OUT / LOVELY / GREEK STYLE / . . .

Hanging's no answer to the plague madam / you'd be hanging everyday / I'm human like us all / we're all the same linked / if you kick one his scream will hit my ears and hurt my mind to think of some poor cunt in shtuck / the way a kitten crying in the night will make you crawl out of your soft pit say what the fuck's up little moggie / free guinness that's the answer and sex instruction initiated by luscious English birds well trained in fuck and suck then instead of marching down the street with weapons of war and little people on the side waving flags / they'll march down with cocks at full alert and straining proud and strong / and promptly get arrested. Still you can't help it / you're drowned in aggro since a kid and dad has fed between your flappy lugs not love but hate / has fed the history of ye old past to give you causes / something to do at night / has woven a tapestry of woe inflicted on him from the dis-tant foggy patch called past. So what else can you do / your tired soggy brain awash with guinness laced with hate . . . I jumped into the bushes and watched the curly mob in a storm of dust go past . . . the palace was on alert . . . the sturdy chiselled chins fresh shaved of our fine and brave John English ready to defend the queen and all her minions who represent all that is fine in this drab of grey / this septic isle . . . *(Chorus of Rule Britannia, Brit-annia rules the waves . . . etc . . .)* eventually got on a train / found one whose carriage wasn't entirely smashed and wrecked and rode in peace to

London's airport skidrow alone and reflective in my thoughts except for some paki in the carriage getting a right kicking for some no doubt vile offence like inadvertently catching the eye of some right gallant son of Tottenham, the kicking lent a rhythmic ritual to my thoughts which were beginning to get formed to take some mighty fine decisions that would shoot me on my path to riches and success sweet smelling pussy and golden arms and lashing tongues. I fell into a kind of reverie . . . I fell asleep and dreamed . . . I saw a dozen pussies on a bed nestled between some soft and squeezy thighs, like little gentle kittens suckling on a mother's teat / their sweet and ivory columns hanging loosely fell apart revealing flowers in a garden that you water and like a randy bee I buzzed from one to tother / their petals gently opened wide / sent forth their perfumes in the air / and as I left they'd close again / and then the next and each one subtly different / each like precious luscious plants / each like a grasping toothless mouth hungry like open beaks of little birds while I, like mother, into their open throats would drop my worm which hungrily and devouringly they'd grasp. Then I awoke / and rudely saw the world just as it is and started on my adventures thrust all young and sweet into the seething heaving heap of world in which I was just a little dot. *(Chorus of airport sounds and noises)* All this confused me / who needs to go / do I do you do he / I decided to stay and see my own sweet land / amend the woes of my own fair state / why split and scarper like ships leaving a sinking rat / I saw myself as king of the western world / but since I needed some refreshment for my trials ahead, I ventured into this little cafe . . . everywhere I looked . . . I witnessed this evidence . . . of the British plague.

Scene Five

Cafe. Chorus of kitchen cafe menu sounds and phrases

EDDY.   One coffee please and croissant and butter

WAITRESS.   Right. Cream?

EDDY.   Please. Where is the butter so I might spread it lavishly and feel its oily smoothness cover the jagged edges of the croissant?

WAITRESS.   Ain't got none. There's a plague on.

EDDY.   Then why serve me the croissant knowing you had no butter?

WAITRESS.   I'll get you something else.

EDDY.   I'll have a cheesecake, what's it like?

WAITRESS.   Our cheesecakes are all made from the nectar of the gods mixed with the dexterous fingers of a hundred virgins who have been whipped with bullrushes grown by the banks of the ganges.

EDDY.   Ok, I'll have one *(she brings it)* . . . I've finished the coffee now and won't have any liquid to wash the cake down with.

WAITRESS. Do you want another coffee?

EDDY. Not want but must not want but have to / you took so long to bring the cake that I finished the coffee so bring another . . .

WAITRESS. OK

EDDY. But bring it before I finish the cheesecake or I'll have nothing to eat with my second cup which I only really want as a masher for the cheesecake

WAITRESS. OK *(to another waitress)* . . . so he came all over your dress . . . .

WAITRESS 2. Yeah

WAITRESS. Dirty bastard.

WAITRESS 2. It was all thick and stringy it took ages to get off / he was sucking me like a madman when my mum walked in

WAITRESS. No! What did she say?

WAITRESS 2. Don't forget to do behind her ears / she always forgets that

WAITRESS. I wish my mum was understanding like that / I haven't sucked a juicy cock for ages, have you?

WAITRESS 2. No, not really, not a big horny stiff thick hot pink one

WAITRESS. What's the biggest you've ever had?

WAITRESS 2. Ten inches

WAITRESS. No!

WAITRESS 2. Yeah, it was all gnarled like an oak with a great big knob on the end

WAITRESS. Yeah?

WAITRESS 2. And when it came, it shot out so much I could have wallpapered the dining room

EDDY. Where's my fucking coffee? I've nearly finished the cheescake and then my whole purpose in life at this particular moment in time will be lost / I'll be drinking hot coffee with nothing to wash it down with

WAITRESS. Here you are, sorry I forgot you!

EDDY. About fucking time!

WAITRESS. Oh shut your mouth, you complaining heap of rat's shit.

EDDY. I'll come in your eyeballs you putrefying place of army gang bang

WAITRESS. You couldn't raise a gallop if I plastred my pussy all over your face, you impotent pooftah bum boy and turd bandit

MANAGER, *her husband*

MANAGER. What's the matter, that you raise your voice you punk and scum / fuck off!

EDDY. No-one talks to me like that

MANAGER. I just did

EDDY. I'll erase you from the face of the earth

MANAGER. I'll cook you in a pie and serve you up for dessert

EDDY. I'll tear you all to pieces, rip out your arms and legs and feed them to the pigs

MANAGER. I'll kick you to death and trample all over you / stab you with carving knives and skin you alive

(They mime fight.)

EDDY. Hit hurt crunch pain stab jab

MANAGER. Smash hate rip tear asunder render

EDDY. Numb jagged glass gouge out

MANAGER. Chair breakhead split fist splatter splosh crash

EDDY. Explode scream fury strength overpower overcome

MANAGER. Cunt shit filth remorse weakling blood soaked

EDDY. Haemhorrage, rupture and swell. Split and cracklock jawsprung and neck break

MANAGER. Cave-in rib splinter oh the agony the shrewd icepick

EDDY. Testicles torn out eyes gouged and pulled strings snapped socket nail scrapped

MANAGER. Bite swallow suck pull

EDDY. More smash and more power

MANAGER. Weaker and weaker

EDDY. Stronger and stronger

MANAGER. Weak

EDDY. Power

MANAGER. Dying

EDDY. Victor

MANAGER. That's it

EDDY. Tada.

WAITRESS. You killed him / I never realised words can kill

EDDY. So can looks

WAITRESS. You killed him / he was my husband

EDDY. I didn't intend to I swear I didn't / he died of shock

WAITRESS.   He was a good man, solid except in his cock but he was good to
me, and now I am alone / who will I have to care for now. Who to wait for at
night while he cleans up our cafe or while he's at the sauna getting relief / who
to cook for or brush the dandruff from his coat and the grease from his hat or
the tramlines from his knickers / who to comfort in the long nights / as he
worries about me / who will put the kids to bed with a gentle cuff as he frolics
after coming home all pissed from the pub and smashes me jokingly on the
mouth / whose vomit will I clean up from the pillow as he heaves up all over
my face on Friday nights after his binge. Whose black uniform will I press in
readiness for his marches down Brixton with the other so noble men of
England / whose photos will I dust in the living room of his heroes, Hitler,
Goebbels, Enoch, Paisley and Maggot not forgetting our dear royals. Is it
worth it any more? / I married a good Englishman / where will I find another
like that? / see what you did / and all over a stupid cheesecake

EDDY.   Wars, my dear, have been fought over less than that

WAITRESS.   I'll never find another like him

EDDY.   Yes you will

WAITRESS.   Where?

EDDY.   Look no further mam than this / your spirits won me / cast thy gaze to
me / my face / and let thine eyes crawl slowly down / that's not a kosher
salami I'm carrying / I'm just pleased to see you / sure I can do like him / po-
lish my knuckleduster / clean **my** pants / I'll give you a kicking with the best if
that's what you really want / you'll have my set of proud photos to dust / I'd
rather treat you fair and square and touch your hair at night and kiss your
sleeping nose / I'll not defile your pillow, but spread violets beneath your feet
/ I'll squeeze your toes at night if they grow cold and when we through rose
gardens walk I'll blow the aphids from your hair / I'll come straight home
from work at night not idle for a pint and all my spunk I'll keep for thee to lash
you with at night as soft and warm as summer showers / I'll leak no precious
drop in the Camden sauna for a fiver ('don't be long dear, others waiting') but
strew the silver load in thee to dart up precious streams / I'll heave my sceptre
into thee / your thighs I'll prise apart and sink like hot stone into butter / into
an ocean of ecstasy for that's what you are to me / an ecstasy of flesh and
blood and fluted pathways softest oils and smells never before uncapped / I'll
turn you upside down and inside out / I'll strip you bare and crawl under your
skin / I'm mad for you / you luscious brat and madam, girl and woman
turned into one / I'll kiss your bum hole like it was the lips of cherubs / I'll
take you love for what you are!

WAITRESS.   You've eased my pain you sweet and lovely boy / I thought I'd
miss him desperately but now I can when looking at you hardly remember
what he looks like. You look so familiar to me though we have never met /
so strange perhaps the true feeling love brings to your heart. The familiar
twang.

EDDY.   I feel the same for you

WAITRESS.   You remind me of someone or something

EDDY.   What, ducky?

WAITRESS.   Oh, nothing

EDDY.   Confess my dear the quandary that doth crease your brow and makes the nagging thought stay in your head, the way an Irish fart hangs in the air long after its creator wends his weary way to Kilburn High Street

WAITRESS.   'Tis nothing sweet but this / I had a kid, just two he were, sweet and blue-eyed just like you / a darling, then one day disaster struck / and don't it just / an August trip to Southend for the day / all hot and sticky with floss and smiling teeth / hankies and braces / start off at Tower Pier excitement, sandwiches and loads of fizzy Tizer

EDDY *(aside)*.   Strange, I love Tizer

WAITRESS.   Then two or three miles out we hit a mine that slunk so steadily up the Thames, like some almighty turd that won't go down no matter how often you flush the chain, so this had stayed afloat, it showed its scarred and raddled cheek from its long buffets round the choppy seas and just by luck as if the fates had ordained us to meet it blew us at the moon / at least it made a hole so large that suddenly the Thames resembled Brighton on a broiling day with heads a bobbing everywhere, my Frank swam back and I clung to a bit of raft but little Tony, for that was his fair name, ne'er did surface up . . . I hope his end was quick

EDDY.   No chance that some local fisherman may have snatched him from the boiling seethe

WAITRESS.   No word, no sign, not even his little corpse did show / I stuck around all night, then as the dawn arose I saw his little oil soaked teddy bear, as if heaved up from deep inside the river's guts. It lay amidst the condoms on the junk filled strand. I took it home and washed it.

EDDY.   That's a sad tale / and I feel grieved for you my dear that woe should strike at one who was so young and fair / and let the others more deserving of fates lash to get away with murder

WAITRESS.   Fate never seems to give out where it's meant but seems to pick you out as from a hat / like bingo and if your number's on it boy you've had it

EDDY.   That little bear you mentioned, sweet . . . may I see the precious relic

WAITRESS.   You really want to?

EDDY.   Yeah, let's have a butchers *(she goes and brings the bear in)* 'tis strange but often times I dreamed of such a thing a little Rufus just like this / I never had one, yet seemed to miss the little furry cuddly thing as if my body knew the feel whereas my mind could not / since then I've always liked small furry things. Come, love, you've had your share of woe and so have I and if fate heaps the shit it also heaps the gold and finding you is like a vein I never dreamed of, so fate's been kind this time / I think we're fated, love don't you?

WAITRESS.   I do, my precious, for once I bless the stars that this time made
me such a man / you've got the same eyes as my Tony — green and jadey
like the sea

EDDY.   Your eyes are like the sunlight in the sea that speckles on the rocks
so deep below / all blue and gold

WAITRESS.   Your face is like all Greek / and carved from ancient marble

EDDY.   Your body feels all soft like puppies, strong as panthers

WAITRESS.   Let's go to bed my sweet

EDDY.   OK

DAD.   Do you think that it could happen
that the curse could come about
that Ed could kill his own dad,
pop into his mothers pants, I had to kick him out

MUM.   That's something we will never know dear
until the day, when suddenly you'll
see quite a different Ed than the one that's known to me

DAD.   You're right, dead right . . . oh Dinah
what did we do that such a curse
should be blasted on the heads of me and you

MUM.   Who knows my dear what evil lies in store
that we are unaware of, did we cause some
grief somewhere, inflict some unhealed sore

DAD.   I've done nothing all my life
I've been an honest Joe
shit on that fortune teller
and his vile and evil joke

MUM.   It's funny that twice we heard it Ted
it's funny that a second time
another face years later should
sound the same old horrid warning line

DAD.   Perhaps we should have told him Dinah
perhaps we ought to tell
our son should know the secret
or we may end up in . . .

MUM.   Hell you mean, you make me laugh
it's over now, it's past,
it can't be now undone with words
fate makes us play the roles we're cast

ACT TWO

Scene One

EDDY.   Ten years have come and gone, scattered their leaves on us / drenched us in blazing sun and rain / toughened my sinews to combat the world. I improved the lot of our fair cafe by my intense efforts, aided of course by my sweet mate / got rid of sloth and stale achievement / which once was thought as normal / I made the city golden era time / the dopes just died away when faced with real octane high power juice / the con men that have tricked you all the while with substitute and fishy watery soup / went out of business and people starved for nourishment brain food and guts just flocked to us / the fat faced bastards you saw sitting on expense accounts and piles / too long defied the needs of our gnawing biting hunger / real food and drink / real substance for the soul / not those decayed and spineless wonders who filled the land / strutting and farting pithy anecdotes at boring dinner parties on profits made by con and cheap / they thought they were the cream and not the sour yuk they really were / we showed them the way / they died in trying to keep up with us / they faded in a heap.

WIFE.   Ten years have flown away as Apollo's Chariot hath with fiery stride lit up our summers, thawed our frosts and kissed our cheeks / ten winters hath the hoary bearded god of ice encased our earth in pinch hard grip of chill / to be kicked out in turn by springs swift feet of Ceres, Pluto, Dionysus / and April brooks do glisten giggling over rocks and reeds so pleased to be set free / ten years this splendid symphony of life hath played its varied song / hath saddened and elated / hath drawn the sap of life into the fiery poppy and frangipani and gripped them in its autumn sleep again / whilst we my man that is and me, for three thousand three hundred and sixty five times did celebrate our own ritual in nights of swooning

EDDY.   While I each day and year have scored another niche into this world of ours / have moved about and jostled / cut a throat or two metaphoric of course and shown how what this world doth crave is power, class and form with a dab of genius now and then. We cured the plague by giving inspiration to our plates / came rich by giving more and taking less / the old style portion control practised by fat thieves went out with us / we put the meat back into the sausage mate / now once more the world will taste good / no more the sawdust and preservative colouring and cat shit that you could better use to fill your walls than line your stomachs / so foul that nations overseas would ban them from their fair stalls and shops lest their strong youth should fall into the listless British trance so often seen in Oxford Street or on the Piccadilly line at 8 a.m. / a nation half asleep and drugged with foul and bestial things poured out of packets / massed up by operators who conspired with commies thick in plot to weaken our defences / feed the nation shit and mothers' crud and watch them crumble down in heaps upon the pavement / then the cunning reds just blow them over skittle like / but now in our great chain we energise the people, give soul food and blistering blast of protein smack / sandwiches the size of fists chock full of juicy smile filled chunks / the nation blinks and staggers back to work on this / not fast / it takes a while to use those muscles starved so long / limp with only holding Daily Mirror race results / and eyes so dim from weekly charting of the pools / we'll get them back to work, no fear though they may die of shock upon the way / we'll drag them out of pubs, their fingers still gripping on the bar they know so well, like babies reluctant to part with mothers tit / it's us that has to do it / rid the world of half-assed bastards clinging to their dark domain and keeping talent out by filling the entrances with their swollen carcasses and sagging mediocrity / let's blow them all sky high, or let us see them simply waste away as the millions come to us.

Chorus sing Jerusalem.

The SPHINX

WIFE.   The plague is not quite over yet. There's still a plague around this city darling that will not go away, caused by some say some evil deed that has not purged itself, but continues to rot away inside the wholesome body of our state / people are dropping like flies / armed killers snipe from the shattered eyes of buildings and death stalks in the foul and pestilent breath of friends whose eyes are drunk with envy and greed at your success / people shake your hand with limp grips as if afraid to catch it. The illness of inertia, and should I shan't I, the country's awash in chemicals that soup the brain to dullness to dull the dullness of grinding hips long bored with ancient habit and lovers are afraid to stroke each others groins lest new laws against the spreading of the plague outlaw them. Masturbating shops line every High Street and the pneumatic drill of strong right wrists ensure a girl a fat living, the country's awash in spunk not threshing and sweetening the wombs of lovers but crushed in kleenex and dead in cubicles with red lights. Meanwhile men in white masks are penetrating the holy crucible where life may have slipped in, and armed with scalpels and suction pumps tear out the living fruit and sluice it down the river of sewage, the future Einsteins, Michelangelos and future Eddys. The blood and plasma of creation is swept and flushed away with gasps of 'don't' inside the tender packages not yet fulfilled.

EDDY.   That's the plague at work all right, there's something rotten in the city that will not die / a sphinx I read stands outside the city walls tormenting all that pass they say and killing those who cannot answer her strange riddle / no doubt she helps to spread the canker and the rot and yet no-one can destroy her

WIFE.   I heard that too, and yet she can at will dissolve herself to air

EDDY.   I'll go and sort her out

WIFE.   Be careful darling / you are all I have

EDDY.   Don't fret, if I've come this far, survived the worst that fate can throw I'll come through this as well don't wait up I may be late but if I'm not back by dawn, I'll meet you in heaven, if not we'll meet in hell!

Scene Two

SPHINX *outside the walls*

SPHINX. Who are you, little man / pip squeak scum / drip off the prick / mistake in the middle of the night / you've come to answer my riddle / the riddle of the sphinx / fuck off you maggot before I tear your head off / rip your eyes out of your head and roast your tongue / you nothing, you man / you insult of nature go now before I lose my cool

EDDY. I'm not afraid of you . . . you old slag / you don't scare Eddy cause Eddy don't scare easy / I've beaten better than you in Singapore brothels / you can only frighten weak men not me / why do you exist to kill men you heap of filth / you detestable disease / because you can't love / loveless you can only terrify man no-one could love you / who could even kiss that mouth of yours when your very breath stinks like a Hong Kong whorehouse when the fleet's in.

SPHINX. You make me laugh you fool man / you should know about brothels, they exist for you to prop up your last fading shreds / men need killing off before they kill off the world / louse, you pollute the earth / every footstep you take rots what's underneath / you turn the seas to dead lakes and the crops are dying from the plague that is man / you are the plague / where are you looking when you should be looking at the ghastly vision in the mirror / the plague is inside you. You make your weapons to give you the strength that you lack / you enslave whip beat and oppress use your guns, chains, bombs, jets, napalm, you are so alone and pathetic, love from you means enslavement, giving means taking, love is fucking, helping is exploiting, you need your mothers you mother fucker, to love is to enslave a woman to turn her into a bearing cow to produce cannon fodder to go on killing / can you ever stop your plague / you're pathetic, unfinished, not like me, never like us, a woman, a sphinx. Women are all sphinx. I have taken the power for all, I am the power / I could eat you alive and blow you out in bubbles / I devour stuff like you . . . oh send me strong men you scrawny nothing / look what they send me / mock up heroes / plastic movie watchers / idoliser of a thousand westerns / punk hero / flaccid man / macho pig / rapist filth and shit / oh nature's mistake in the ghastly dawn of time / when women were women, androgynous and whole and could reproduce themselves but somewhere and some time a reptile left our bodies, it crawled away and became man, but it stole our little bag of seed and ever since the little reptile has been trying to crawl back, but we don't want it anymore, all we need is your foul little seed, you gnat . . . something that takes you 30 seconds of your life and us 9 months we create build nourish care for, grow bigger and fat and after we suckle and provide. While you dig in the earth for treasure, play your stupid male games / go you biped of dirt / just a prick followed by a heap of filth, I feel sorry for you / I really feel for you / I've eaten enough men this week / so go / fuck off / stink scum dirt shit / go, before I tear you to pieces / go and plot and scheme, hurt, exploit and rape, oppress and wound, make a few more evil laws you shrivel of flesh, you poor unreliable penis. You have not even our capacity for passion . . . I could come ten times to your one / wanna try big boy? You are from my rib mister / me from you? what a joke / woman was Adam / she was the earth, woman is the tide / woman is in the movement of the universe / our bodies obey the phases of the moon . . . our breasts swell and heave and our rich blood surges forth to tell us we are part of the movement of nature / what signs do you have? / How do you know that you are even alive? / Do you bleed / do you feel the kicking in your womb / does a mouth draw milk from your soft breast / can you tell the future / can you do anything? What signs do you have / a date with death / the hour you must attack / unable to create you must destroy / I am the earth / I am the movement of the universe / I am liquid, fire and all elements / my voice rises octaves high and communicates with the spirits of the dead / my skin is soft and velvet and desirable to those with rough faces and bodies hard and muscled to labour, to toil across the face of the earth for us / the goodness of life / woman / we / sex / sphinx, the grand and majestic cunt, the great mouth of life / the dream of men in their aching lonely nights / the eternal joy that men die for and envy and emulate / what they sicken for and crave for and go insane for / so go, you are small, insignificant, piss off you worm or I'll break your teeth and pull out your fingers / go fuck yourself or stick a bomb up your fucking asshole you heap of murdering bastard shit filth . . . go, you make me vomit.

EDDY.   Without me you are nothing / without me you wouldn't exist without me you are an empty screaming hole

SPHINX.   You what! You think I need you. I need milk but do I go to bed with a cow. I'll farm and fertilise you and keep you in pens where you will do no harm / now go boy, I am getting aroused, be grateful that for some reason I feel for your pathetic attempts at heroism

EDDY.   I want to answer your riddle

SPHINX.   Then you must know that those that can't answer it die, and then if you can't I will kill you, I will tear your cock off with my teeth before I eat you up

EDDY.   With pleasure / if I answer it / what do I gain /

SPHYINX.   You can kill me

EDDY.   Then I will cut off your head for women talk too much

SPHINX.   I agree. You're a brave little fart. So here goes: what walks on four legs in the morning, two legs in the afternoon and three legs in the evening?

EDDY.   Man! In the morning of his life he is on all fours, in the afternoon when he is young he is on two legs and in the evenings when he is erect for his women he sprouts the third leg

SPHINX.   You bastard, you've used trickery to find out the riddle

EDDY.   No, just reason. All right, sorry to have to do this, I was growing quite fond of you.

SPHINX.   I don't care any more / to tell you the truth I was getting bored with scaring everyone to death and being a sphinx / OK cut it off and get it over with.

He cuts off her head.

Scene Three

EDDY.   She would put you off women for life / but not me / I love a woman / I love her / I just love and love and love her / and even that one / I could have loved her / I love everything that they possess / I love all their parts / I love every part that moves / I love their hair and their neck / I love the way they walk across the kitchen to put the kettle on / in that lazy familiar way / I love them when they open their eyes in the morning / I love their baby soft skin / I love their voices / I love their smaller hands than mine / I love lying on them and them on me / I love their soft breasts / I love their eyelashes and their noses / their teeth and their shoulders / and their giggles / and their desperate passions and their liquids and their breath against yours in the night / and their snores / and their leg across yours and their feet in the morning and I love their bellies and thighs and the way each part fits into mine / and love the way my part fits into them / and love her sockets and joints and ball bearings / and love her hip bone and her love soaked parts that want me / I love her seasons and love her sleeping and love her walking and speaking and whispering and loving and singing and love her back and her bum nestled into you and you become an armchair / and love her for taking me in / and giving me a home for my searing agonies / my lusts / my love / my dreams / my sweetness / my honey / my peace of mind / and love pouring all my love into her with open eyes and love our fatigue and love her knees and shoulder blades and pimples and love her waiting for me and love her soothing me as I tell her about my day's battles in the world — and love and love and love her and her and!

WIFE *enters*

WIFE.   Well done my sweet, now all will be well / my hero . . . yes you are / my brave and shining knight / my lion, yes! And I'm your mate / my brave and gentle lion / and now to celebrate let's have your dear old pa and ma to dine and reconcile the fairy tales and woes of past and be all gooey nice together in family bliss

EDDY.   I have to laugh when I think of my soppy mum and dad / locked up in council bliss / and £40 a week driving a 38 from Putney down to Waltham Cross and getting clobbered each Saturday night

WIFE.   Invite them over Ed, to share just once our colour TV, hi-fi, home movies showing us in fair Ibiza and Thebes, of you diving in the bight blue cobalt sea, your smiling new capped teeth all sparkling in the brilliant sun, invite them to partake of our deep leather sofas / succulent wines / show our video that records those programmes that you wish to view when after working late at night in selfless graft you sit with dog and slipper by your feet . . . let them enjoy the comfort of central heated bathroom . . . no more the cold ass on a plastic seat but wool covered and pipes all steaming hot, of stairs thick gloved in pile so soft that each tread is like a luscious meadow. Would they not like a slumberdown or even our soft waterbed which thrusts our pelvises so sweetly swished together, needlepoint shower show your mum the joys of kitchen instant disposal waste, no washing up, just time to enjoy our super apple pie.

EDDY.   I'll send the chauffeur down to pick them up / that's if my dad has rid himself of that old hoary myth that like a louse ate inside his nut, to tell him of patricide and horrid incest / or subtitled could be called the story of a mother fucker / a tale for kiddiwinks to send them mad to bed and cringe at shadows in the night, and in their later years to bung good gelt to shrinks in Harley Street.

WIFE.   When you told me that story Ed / I could not believe that grown ups still could set such store by greasy gypsies in a booth / and to kick you out all young and pink into the seething world while you were wet behind the lugs / maybe 'twas a ruse to get you out the nest

EDDY.   Who knows my dear the wily minds of cruddy mums and dads whose heads chock full of TV swill, the pools and read your own horoscope / who believe in anything they read that comes so fluent forth from out the gushy asses of the turds in fleeting street / so what, it put me on the springboard young and lively and I learned how to jack knife into the surging tide with all the best.

WIFE.   You're tuf that's what my love / you're a survivor in the swilling mass of teeth and knives and desperate eyes all anxious to carve out their pound of flesh / you did it and you're still a beaut / still lovely brown and svelte / success has not paunched you or stuck a fat ass on your hips or burnt an ulcer in your gut / or made your mouth a stinking ashtray where fat cigars hang like a turd that cannot be expelled / but hangs on till the end / your sweet and honey breath / your tongue's not coated with the slime of ten course meals taken with other con artists who flash their gaudy rings and thick as pig shit wives who sit at home and wank or play some bridge with other dozy bags whose only exercise is stretching out an arm to screech out taxi outside Harrods / you're sweet and your body's like a river, flowing, flowing, flowing into me / it moves like a flowing river . . . your streaming muscles carry me along your river, along your soft and hard and flowing river / when I'm in your arms I'm carried along this endless stream and then I reach the sea, I'm swept up by your sea, I'm carried by a wave, I'm threshed up in your wave and then set down again only to be re-gathered up as your volcanic wave gathers me as a piece of ocean, as your sweet lustful pangs gather up its morsel I'm swept up, I'm gathered up, I'm sucked up and spun along a raging storming river . . . I love your body, I love your fingers round and round and tearing and gripping and finding and searching and twisting and gathering me for your sweet lustful pangs . . . and then and then and then . . . your body is like a tree . . . like branches twisting and breaking . . . like a wave like a wind, like an animal like a lion . . . ferocious and sweet lustful pangs grow bigger darling . . . as they grow bigger to make your sweet spunk flow . . . they grow bigger and the lion's breath is hot and the grip on me is growing tight and more ferocious and then and then I know . . . that you tremble, you shake, you quiver, you thrash . . . oh the river flows, oh . . . it flows, oh it floods through me . . . as you tremble your quiver is shot into me . . . oh I am flowing with the river in the wet and warm and succulent flow . . . you turn me into a flow and flood me . . . and the shivering and the quivering and the shaking and the trembling, softly softly . . . softly goes as the storm passes slowly . . . goes . . . slowly . . . rumbling into the distance . . . slowly goes the breath less hot, but soft and silky and sweat on your back and silky on your thighs and warm between our thighs . . . oh / life my love / oh love my precious / oh sweet my honey / oh heaven my angel / oh darling my husband.

EDDY.   But soft my darling wife / what noise is that / it must be my cruddy mum and dad / who interrupt your lovely flow of gob rich thick and pearly verbs that send my blood a racing to my groin so I might manufacture love wet tides.

Scene Four

MUM *and* DAD *enter.*

DAD.   Look how he's got on / you really got on well son / I'm proud of ya. He's got class and qualities drawn from me.

MUM.   From me more, his mum whom he did love not this wet fart that calls himself his dad.

DAD.   Don't talk like that in front of Eddy's wife you sloppy titted, slack assed lump, you raving scrawny dried up witch

MUM.   Don't talk to me about my body / age has withered my soft beauty but you will need cremating since your poisoned flesh would cause pollution in the earth and make widespread crop failures you're death on two varicosed legs and a hernia belt

DAD.   I've got no words for you Dot . . . since you were gang banged by that bunch of drunken darkies . . . a dozen it were, if I counted right, whose swollen truncheons flashed their golden sprints of foam into the sulphurous and heavy night, since that bad time you've not been right in ye old bonce . . . I know that night was dark for you in double horror and I fear that it may be the cause of your unseemly evil tongue that like a poisoned snake doth linger under filthy damp and rotting stone.

EDDY.   Hello dad, hellow mum — good to see ya again . . .

MUM.   Oh Ed, it looks really lovely, and this is your lovely wife / oh! how lovely, oh, she's nice

WIFE.   Why thank you, I think you're very charming yourself

MUM.   Oh thank you. You are nice, have a nice day, you're welcome

WIFE.   Please feel free, make yourself at home, how very nice to meet you. Have you had a good journey? How is everyone at home. Isn't the weather cold now. It will soon be winter. You're looking so young. You really look well. You've lost weight. Are you going away this summer! Do you use fablon in your kitchen?

MUM.   You've a lovely home, it's really lovely, just lovely. Some people are lucky, some people have all the fun. Some mothers do have 'em. Mind you, I mean, it goes to show, well it does. Idle hands make wicked thoughts. He's all right, really, underneath . . . when you get to know him, he's lovely, have you been away this year? Water off a duck's back dear.

EDDY.   So what's the news my folks / my flesh and blood / chip off the old / apple of your / say what goes on in my old neighbourhood / where once rank violence stalked the dirty streets and filthy yobbos hung round the corners of old pubs like flies on dead carrion / say can you still walk down the streets at night? Or do you macaroni in your pants at every shadow that stalks out lest it be some Mcdougal out to line his coat with other's hard earned gelt . . . around this manor there's peace my folks. Move out that council flat where urchins' piss does spray the lift which takes you to your eyrie on the 25th floor and move in with us, or do you still fear that old curse / that bunch of gypsy bollocks, that you so avidly did gulp / though secretly me thinks you used that as a ruse, to clear me out the womb and save yourself some L.s.d. / you always said I'd eat you out of house and home / round here only the poodles drop their well turned turds in little piles so neat. And au pair girls go pushing little Jeremys into the green and flowery parks / no ice-cream vans come screaming round this manor / all's quiet / just the swish on the emerald lawns close cropped like the shaven heads of astronauts / and in the quiet of the evening silly chit chat from the strangled vocal chords of well heeled neighbours rises from the gardens as they wolf down in the summer nights a half a dozen gin and tonics. Nicely tired from a hard days graft of thieving in the city. So come and stay. You're welcome and bring the cat as well, we've always got room for moggie.

DAD.   Nah son but thanks and double ta. You're very kind to us . . . how thoughtful / bless you, you're welcome, have a nice day, but we're used to wot we got, can you teach an old dog new tricks, a bit long in the tooth you're as old as you feel, and I feel like a worn out old fart . . . we know the familiar faces / our rotten neighbours / the geezer who collects the payments on the fridge and on the telly every week / meals on wheels that daily calls now that we're getting older, all familiar trappings that have trapped us / now that our useful working life has been sucked dry by the state we get a little pension and some security for which I sign / now that my boss god bless him sits back fat and greasy / not that I mind, he got it by hard graft and cunning / good luck to him / he gave me fifty quid when I retired, handsome and a watch with 15 jewels / right proud I was / so what I got asbestos in my lung / so what I got coal dust in my blood / so what I got lead poisoning in my brain / so what I got shot nerves from the machines / so what I lost two fingers in the press / so what I'm going deaf from the steel mills / so what I lost a lung for our old king in Dunkirk / I'd do it again / yes I would I tell ya / so what I got fuck all for it from our fair state / so what they're gliding past in their Rolls Royces / and their fat little kids come tumbling out on piggy little legs / so what they thieve and murder and get away with it / so what our lovely royals pay no tax / they're figureheads mate / so what I starve waiting for your cheque which sometimes you forget to send if you are busy entertaining, when you forget your old ma and pa . . . son!

MUM. Don't listen Ed, he's gone a bit in the nut since they retired him / all he does is grouse and quail. When you complain remember others worse off than you / I think of mothers whose sweet fruit of their most holy wombs / those warm and precious sacks of giggling joy, who have been snatched by sex mad fiends. They stalk around the town . . . there are so many around / you cannot pick up the daily snot picker these days without seeing between the tits and race results the photos of the burns and scalds and broken limbs . . . the staring eyes of kids / how one is burnt by fag ends / others punched black and blue / screams in the night / neighbours too scared or fastened to Hawaii Five-O to receive the bloated cries that stab through the walls like an open hand saying help me / others, babies with broken lips, their little ribs all smashed by dads who have caught the British plague that cements their heads and puts vitriol inside their hearts / some kids chained to their beds for hours at a time and others crawling in shit and piss . . . and whack and zunk goes mum and splatter back hand crack goes dad . . . one kid's nipples almost burnt off . . . what about the dad who picked up his small innocent and smashed his head against the wall, until his brains seeped out . . . what dreams did that kid have as his grey thoughts ran down the wallpaper . . . and then the judge says . . . 'off you go, you are basically a good character . . . and then he's off to celebrate in the nasty pub with his old lady . . . and up and down the length and breadth the straps are out and babies, bairns and kids are straightened out, lashed out, whipped and made to obey, the nations full of perverts if you ask me / the plague still flourishes mate.

EDDY. The plague mum / the plague is still about? You never did nuffin like that to me / you only gave me muffins and jam / swaddles of lovey love and spoiling and playing and story telling. And swishing my pillow and a ride on dad's back and chase around the garden, and a three wheel bike. You only gave me ten slices of toast every morning and marmite after school . . . I looked all bisto like, and like those kids whose shoes have a long way to go I was put on a path called bliss with jammy mouth and sticky doughnut figers / a dad who put me on the crossbar of his bike and never once introduced the back of his hand to my bonce not once opened his eyes wide and hatefilled and sought to venge some filthy taste for colouring my flesh in chartreuse green or bruisy blue. No! We'd race across the municpal lido. How long can you stay under. Dandy and the Beano each week and even the Film Fun as well.

DAD. You were loved son / we wanted to give you love / we luved ya kid. You know . . . like open hands gripping your shoulders and a squeeze at the end . . . palm on your head and ruffling your hair, a clenched fist and a slow tap on the chin . . . like chin-up when you didn't pass your eleven-plus 'cause you were a dummy . . . I didn't want you to hate us.

EDDY.   Hate? I never used that word my folks, only pocket money each week five bob and Sat morn flicks. Do you mean to say you loved me because you were afraid I'd hate you. Cause the gypsy's curse rang in your ears. Let's smother him with spoiling and cuddling so he won't want to hurt his old dad, you make me laugh . . . you would have loved me the same without the rotten curse / I'm your flesh and blood, it's natural

DAD and MUM.   But you're not our son, son.

EDDY.   SHIT GIVE UP THE GEN / SPILL YOUR GUTS / OPEN YOUR NORTH AND SOUTH AND LET ROLL THE TURDS BEFORE I PONEY MY Y FRONTS. IN OTHER VERBS OPEN YOUR CAKE-HOLE AND UTTER. LET ME EARWIG YOUR HOBSONS. NOT YOUR SON. OH BOLLOCKS AND CRACKLOCK.

WIFE.   Don't say that he ain't your real produce of your blood swept thighs, not shoved out of your guts in warm sticky afterbirth, not the sparkle in his dad's eye in the glinting night when his pa heaved apart his woman's limbs and unloaded a binful of hot spunk, not eyed her like a lodestone or a star, or a jewel in the corner of his eye not breathed hard or pulse raced to produce this lovely hunk of super delicious wondrous beefy darling spunky guy / not seen you walking from behind and wanted to grasp your arse and deliver the mail up your wet and wondrous letter-box?

MUM.   Nah! 'Fraid not!

WIFE.   Oh fuck.

EDDY.   So what if I'm adopted / who gives a monkey's tit.

DAD.   Like this it was. Cries and groans, shouts and shrieks. I was fishing by Wapping, just down from the Prospect of Whitby . . . a peaceful Sunday (you were fished out, what a find, what I prayed for, a son) threw my line, the big steamers going out to Southend. The old Tower Bridge opening up to allow the steamers' funnels through like some big lazy East End tart from Cable Street opening her thighs . . . on the deck in the sun the people of Bow, Whitechapel and Islington in their cheese-cutters and chokers, all doing a bit of a dance on the deck, the streamers flickering, the guinness pouring . . . us waving from the shore as the old steamer cuts through the scummy old Thames and sends the swell over to us and makes our little boats kneel and bob as she passes by. When all of a sudden boy / the sun's up high, Hitler's just topped hisself. It's hot. Churchill's in command, there's peace at last. Twenty million dead / including my two boys, the radio plays we'll meet again and mares eat oats and does eat oates and little lambs eat ivy, remember. Well all of a sudden in that hot August afternoon no bananas in the shops and coupons for four oz of sweets each week, pictures of Auschwitz just come out / thousands of bodies like spaghetti all entwined / all done in the name of Adolf / all of a sudden in the hot blue day . . . they're all swimming look at them, look at all that blood and oil, bad mix, the sky turned black. What a terrific hell of a bang, and soot is dropping all over us plus bits of people, all the fish dropped dead, from shock, hey let's shlap them out. Look let's get some help, they're all in the water. Some jerry ball of hate stacked full of painful promise and carrying the names of the future dead blew the Southend tripper to the moon and down they fell in a deadly mash of guinness and gold flake . . . come on mate . . . 'I'll give you a hand'. We pulled them in all night, the others just bloated up like fun-fair freaks. Come on mum, don't fret, ere have a cuppa, where's your little Johnnie? . . . now, now he'll be all right, can he swim? No . . . oh. We'll find him . . . won't we lads . . . we'll find the little bleeder . . . shine your torch over here Bert, yeah, there's an old lady, give us your hand love, I'll pull you in . . . oh no, just a stump, she left it in the water . . . what bastard could do this . . . more blankets . . . bring more tea . . . there's just not enough of us . . . there's not enough people to help, who does this to people! What sick perverted bastard started all this shit . . . if he was in front of me, I would take a butcher's fucking knife and carve him slowly bit by fucking dirty piece and feed it to the river rats and any cunt that supports him, I'd fucking throw them in acid baths . . . when all had gone and the dawn arose we saw what seemed a little doll clinging to a piece of wood but on closer butchering revealed a little bugger of about two he were, struggling like the fuck and gripping in his other paw a greasy old big bear, which no doubt helped to keep him up. We threw the bear back in the slick, and lifted the toddler out all dripping wet and covered in oil looking like a darkie so, no-one about we took him home and washed him / he was a beaut / and mum was double chuffed to see a little round soft ball of warm goo goo / don't want to give him up quoth Dinah, must we she said. Nah, I said his mum will think he's dead anyway / so let her go on thinking it / but think our Dinah rightly slurps of how its real mum will fret and pine and waste away and mourn for her sweet lovely soft flesh of her own / all right I says we'll keep him for one day only and then give him back. A day turned into two / then after a week we thought the shock now would be too great and that the true mum would be adjusted to her sad loss.

WIFE.   Oh shit and piss and fuck. I just pissed in my pants.

She faints.

EDDY.   My dearest wife and now my mum, it seems, this lady was the very one whose baby you snatched / she told me the selfsame and bitter tale of how she lost her Tony and if you found him then I am he, he whom you found that belonged to her was me. The he you stole and gave to her did once belong to she . . . nice to see ya, have a nice day, so I am the squelchy mass of flesh that issued from out the loins of my dear wife / oh rats of shit / you opened a right box there didn't you, you picked up a stone that was best left with all those runny black and horrid things intact and not nibbling in my brain. So the man I verballed to death was my real pop / the man to whom my words like hard edged shrapnel razed his brain / was the source of me, oh stink / warlock and eyes break shatter, cracker and splatter . . . ! / Who laughs? Me who wants to clean up the city / stop the plague destroy the sphinx / me was the source of all the stink / the man of principle is a mother fucker / oh no more will I taste the sweetness of my dear wife's pillow . . . no more . . . no more . . . so I left my cosy and love filled niche now so full of horror / foul incest and babies on the way which if they come will no doubt turn into six fingered horrors with two heads / poor Eddy. Oh this madness twisting my brain / I walked through the plague rot streets and witnessed the old and the broken / the funny faces staring out of the dead vinyl flats / the flickering shadows of the TV tube / I sat in cafes and thought of my desirable lovely succulent and honey filled wife and as I sat and stared at the rheumy faces and the dead souls with their real wives who were plastered forever in casts of drab compromise, my own wife seemed like a princess / I fastened her face on the horizon like the rising moon and stared forever into space / and when the cafe closed I sat and stared forever and forever, ran through in my mind every combination of her face and smile and eyes and twists and curves of her lips, I sat and projected her picture on the moon and pored through every page of our life together like a great holy bible of magic events I examined every feature of her landscape and ate up every part of her and loved every part whose sum total made up this creature, my wife. And then the moon turned as red as blood / the clouds raced across her face and became her hair and then her eyes and the wind pulled her hair over her face / like it did when we walked together through the fields and the forests, when the trees shivered and the sun kissed us and the universe wrapped us round in a cloak of stars and rain and crushed grass and ice-creams and teas and clenched fingers / hold on to me / hold on to me and I will hold on to you and I'll never let you go, hold on to me, does it matter that you are my mother, I'll love you even if I am your son / do we cause each other pain, do we kill each other, do we maim and kill, do we inflict vicious wounds on each other. We only love so it doesn't matter mother, mother it doesn't matter. Why should I tear my eyes out Greek style, why should you hang yourself / have you seen a child from a mother and son / no. Have I? No. Then how do we know that it's bad / should I be so mortified? Who me. With my nails and fingers plunge in and scoop out those warm and tender balls of jelly quivering dipped in blood. Oedipus how could you have done it, never to see your wife's golden face again, never again to cast your eyes on her and hers on your eyes. What a foul thing I have done, I am the rotten plague, tear them out Eddy, rip them out, scoop them out like ice-cream, just push the thumb behind the orb and push, pull them out and stretch them to the end of the strings and then snap! Darkness falls. Bollocks to all that. I'd rather run all the way back and pull back the sheets, witness my golden bodied wife and climb into her sanctuary, climb all the way in right up to my head and hide away there and be safe and comforted. Yeh I wanna climb back inside my mum. What's wrong with that. It's better than shoving a stick of dynamite up someone's ass and getting a medal for it. So I run back. I run and run and pulse hard and feet pound, it's love I feel it's love, what matter what form it takes, it's love I feel for your breast, for your nipple twice sucked / for your belly twice known / for your hands twice caressed / for your breath twice smelt, for your thighs, for your cunt twice known, once head first once cock first, loving cunt holy mother wife / loving source of your being / exit from paradise / entrance to heaven.

END